Introduction to Surveillance & Insurance Claims Investigations, F.S. 493, Rules, Regulations, Laws & Procedures

First Edition

Table of Contents

	Page
Chapter One State Statute 493 Private Investigations	3-17
Chapter Two Sponsorship Relationship	18-23
Chapter Three Professional Ethics	24-32
Chapter Four Legal Issues	33-41
Chapter Five The Private Investigator	42-51
Chapter Six Locate Investigations	52-58
Chapter Seven Surveillance Investigations	59-81
Chapter Eight Equipment of the Professional Investigator	82-87
Chapter Nine Safe Guarding and Restriction of Information	88-92
Chapter Ten Report Writing	93-111
Chapter Eleven Common Investigations & Reports	112-135
Chapter Twelve Being a Witness	136-139
Chapter Thirteen Terrorism Today	140-146
Chapter Fourteen Statement Taking	147-180
Chapter Fourteen Being Ready for a PI Position	181-185

Chapter One
State Statute 493 Private Investigations

    I.   Law
    II.   Regulated Activity
    II.   Types of Licenses
    III. In-House Investigators
    IV.   Training and Test requirements
    V.   Firearms
            a. Firearms Training
            b. Use of Force
    VI.   Sponsorship of Interns
    VII. Company ID Cards
    VIII. Applying for a License
            a. Cancellation/Inactivation of Licensing
    IX.   Agency Advertising
    X.   Other prohibited Acts
            a. Use of State Seal
            b. Use of Badge
    XI.   Unlawful Symbols of Authority
    XII. The Department of Agriculture & Consumer Services
    XIII. Disciplinary Actions/ Penalties
    XIV. Confidentiality
    XV.   Divulging Investigative Information

1. Law – Florida Statutes 493

The following explanations of the law are presented to assist applicants and licensees in understanding the basic requirements and restrictions of Chapter 493, Florida Statutes. Please note that this section does not constitute the entirety of the law. Individuals seeking a more comprehensive understanding of the law are directed to carefully read and study Chapter 493, Florida Statutes, as well as Chapter 5N-1, Florida Administrative Code.

Regulated Activity – Private Investigation
Definition — the investigation by a person or persons for the purpose of obtaining information with reference to any of the following matters:

a. Crime or wrongs done or threatened against the United States or any state or territory of the United States, when operating under express written authority of the governmental official responsible for authorizing such investigation.

b. The identity, habits, conduct, movements, whereabouts, affiliations, associations, transactions, reputation, or character of any society, person, or group of persons.

c. The credibility of witnesses or other persons.

d. The whereabouts of missing persons, owners of abandoned property or escheated property, or heirs to estates.

e. The location or recovery of lost or stolen property.

f. The causes and origin of, or responsibility for, fires, libels, slanders, losses, accidents, damage, or injuries to real or personal property.

g. The business of securing evidence to be used before investigating committees or boards of award or arbitration or in the trial of civil or criminal cases and the preparation therefore.

h. A Class "C" or Class "CC" licensee may perform bodyguard services without obtaining a Class "D" license.

Types of Licenses

a. Private Investigator — Class "C" license — Any individual, except an "in-house" investigator, who performs investigative services must have a Class "C" Private Investigator license and must own or be employed by a licensed Class "A" Private Investigative Agency or Class "AA" or "AB" branch office. Class "C" licensees may not engage in investigative services except through a licensed agency.
Class "C" licensees may not subcontract.

b. Private Investigator Intern — Class "CC" license — Any individual who performs investigative services as an intern under the direction and control of a designated sponsoring Class "C" licensee or designated sponsoring Class "M" or "MA" Agency Manager licensee. Class "CC" licensees may not subcontract; they must work for a Class "A" agency or branch office.

c. Private Investigative Agency — Class "A" license — Any company that engages in business as an investigative agency must possess a Class "A" license. A Class "A" license is valid for only one location. A Class "A" agency cannot subcontract with a Class "C" Private Investigator or Class "CC" Private Investigator Intern, but that agency may subcontract with another Class "A" agency.

d. Branch Office — Class "AA" license — Each branch office of a Class "A" agency shall have a Class "AA" license.

e. Agency Managers — Class "M" or "MA" license — Any individual who performs the services of a manager for a Class "A" Investigative Agency or a Class "AA" Branch Office must have a Class "M" or "MA" Agency Manager license. A Class "C" licensee may be designated as a manager in lieu of the Class "M" or "MA" license. Class "M" or "MA" licensees cannot subcontract; they must work for a Class "A" Private Investigative Agency.

f. Each agency or branch office shall designate a minimum of one appropriately licensed individual to act as manager, directing the activities of the Class "C" or Class "CC" employees.

g. The owner of a Class "A" Private Investigative Agency who is licensed as a Class "C" Private Investigator can designate himself/herself as the agency manager and does not have to apply for Class "MA" licensure.

h. All licenses are valid for two (2) years, except Class "A", Class "AB", or Class "AA" agency licenses, which are valid for three (3) years, unless suspended or revoked by the Division of Licensing. The Division sends renewal notices/applications to each licensee approximately 90 days prior to the date on which that licensee's license is scheduled to expire. However, it is the responsibility of each licensee to renew his/her license in a timely manner, even if the licensee does not receive that renewal notice.

i. The Class "C" Private Investigator license or Class "CC" Private Investigator Intern license or Class "M" or "MA" Agency Manager license must be in the possession of the individual licensee while engaged in regulated activities.

In-House Investigators – No license required
Definition — An unarmed investigator who is solely, exclusively, and regularly employed as an investigator in connection with the business of his/her employer when such employer does not provide, or advertise as providing, investigative services for a fee. An unlicensed investigator may not provide investigative services to any person or business other than his/her employer.

Example: An individual may be employed to investigate matters specifically related to his/her employer's business such as employee theft, background checks on potential employees, etc.

Example: Investigators working in-house for a Class "A" Agency must have a Class "C" license and are not exempt under Section 493.6102(3), F.S.

Training and Test Requirements

a. An applicant for a Class "CC" Private Investigator Intern License is not expected to have investigative experience. Internship is intended to serve as a learning period during which the intern works under the direction and guidance of a trained and licensed investigator. However, there are training and examination requirements for Class "CC" applicants.

b. **Effective September 1, 2008**, an applicant for a Class "CC" Private Investigator Intern license must complete a 40-hour training course. This course, which is offered by a state university or by a school, community college, college, or university under the purview of the Department of Education, focuses on general investigative techniques and Chapter 493, F. S. The applicant must also pass an initial examination. The course and the examination must be completed prior to applying for the license. The applicant must submit documentation confirming that he/she has completed the course and passed the exam with the application for licensure.

c. The 40–hour training course can be administered to students in a number of ways: in a traditional classroom setting, through an online course made available via the Internet, or through a home study correspondence training course.

d. If a Class "CC" license becomes invalid as a result of expiration or administrative action and remains invalid for more than one year, the person applying for re-licensure must retake both the training and the two examinations. *Section 493.6203(6)(a) and (b), F.S.*

e. An applicant for a Class "C" license shall have two (2) years of lawfully gained, verifiable, full-time experience or training in one, or a combination of more than one, of the following:

1. Private investigative work or related fields of work that provided equivalent experience or training.

2. College course work related to criminal justice, criminology, or law enforcement administration, or successful completion of any law enforcement-related training received from any federal, state, county, or municipal agency, except that no more than one (1) year may be used from this category.

3. Work as a Class "CC" licensed intern.
Example: An applicant for Class "C" licensure cannot claim investigative experience obtained when the applicant or the employer/sponsor was not properly licensed because this would be unlawfully gained experience.

f. **Effective January 1, 2008,** an applicant for the Class "MA", Class "M", or Class "C" license must pass an examination that covers the provisions of Chapter 493, F.S. This examination is administered by the Department or by a provider approved by the Department. The applicant must pass the examination prior to applying for licensure; proof of successful completion of the exam must be submitted with the application. Applications received by the division prior to 1/1/08 are not required to submit proof of completion of the exam.

g. This examination requirement will not apply to individuals who already hold a Class "MA", Class "M", or Class "C" license as of January 1, 2008.

h. If a Class "MA", Class "M", or Class "C" license becomes invalid as a result of expiration or administrative action and remains invalid for more than one year, the person applying for re-licensure must take and pass the examination a second time.

Firearms

a. A Class "C" Private Investigator or Class "CC" Private Investigator Intern must obtain a Class "G" Statewide Firearm License in order to carry a firearm in the course of his/her duties. A Class "C" or Class "CC" licensee has authority to carry a .38 caliber revolver; or a .380 caliber or a 9-millimeter semiautomatic pistol; or a .357 caliber revolver with .38 caliber ammunition, while performing duties authorized under Chapter 493, Florida Statutes. No licensee may carry more than two (2) firearms upon his/her person when performing his/her duties. A licensee may carry only a firearm of the specific type and caliber with which he/she is qualified in accordance with the firearms training requirements. Licensees may not carry a concealed firearm under the authority of a concealed weapon license obtained pursuant to Section 790.06, Florida Statutes, while engaged in activities regulated by Chapter 493.

b. A Class "C" Private Investigator, a Class "CC" Private Investigator Intern, a Class "M" or "MA" Manager, age twenty-one (21) years or older, who possesses a Class "G" Statewide Firearm License may carry a concealed firearm if required by his/her duties AND if the armed duty assignment is made and approved by his/her employer (the licensed agency). The Class "G" license is valid throughout the state. Open-carry of a firearm is not permitted at any time.

c. Licensed agencies shall allow licensed employees to use only standard (factory) ammunition of a type and load which is appropriate for the location and duty requirements of armed employees, with the exception of the following types of prohibited ammunition:

1. Glaser-type or any other pre-fragmented type bullets
2. Exploding bullets
3. Full-metal-jacket (fmj)/full-metal-case
(fmc) bullets (except this type may be used in semiautomatic pistols only).
4. Teflon-coated (ktw-type) or any other type of armor-piercing bullets
5. Full wad-cutter bullets (except on firing range)
6. Reloads (except on firing range)

Firearms Training

a. An applicant for a Class "G" Statewide Firearm license must have a minimum of twenty-eight (28) hours of range and classroom training within the past twelve (12) months. This training must be taught and administered by a Class "K" Firearms Instructor.

b. Class "G" licensees must obtain four (4) hours of firearms range recertification training during each year of the 2-year licensure period (eight hours of total training required for recertification/renewal). Range recertification must be taught and administered by a Class "K" Firearms Instructor. Renewal of the Class "G" license will be denied if a licensee has failed to fulfill the four (4) hour annual training requirement. If the 4 hours of annual training is not completed each year during the 2-year licensing period, the individual must re-take the training required at initial licensure.

Example: A licensee who is issued his Class "G" license on March 1, 2009, which expires February 28, 2011, must receive four (4) hours of firearms recertification training between March 1, 2009, and February 28, 2010, and four (4) hours between March 1, 2010, and February 28, 2011.

c. Investigative agencies are required to notify the Division of Licensing within five (5) working days of any discharge of a firearm by an employee other than on a range during range training. Reports are to be made on a form prescribed by the department. This form can be obtained from any division regional office.

Example: An accidental discharge by an employee must be reported.

d. Deadly force may be used only in the defense of one's self or another from imminent serious bodily harm. The discharge of a firearm under any other circumstances, such as firing a warning shot, is grounds for disciplinary action, including revocation of the Class "G" license.

Use of Force

a. Private investigators are not law enforcement officers and are not granted any police powers regarding arrest or use of force.

b. Deadly force may never be used by a private investigator except in self-defense or defense of another from imminent death or great bodily harm. The use of deadly force to protect property or to prevent property loss is prohibited by law.

c. Non-deadly force may be used by private investigators to the extent necessary for self-defense or defense of another against the use of unlawful force or to prevent or terminate trespass or "interference" with persons he/she has a legal duty to protect.

d. Firing a warning shot for any reason, including an attempt to stop a person suspected of the commission of a crime, is prohibited.

Sponsorship of Interns

a. Only a Class "C", Class "MA", or Class "M" licensee may sponsor a Class "CC" Private Investigator Intern.

b. An internship may not commence until the intern is licensed, or has submitted a completed application, and the sponsor has submitted the notice of intent to sponsor to the department. Such notice shall be on a form provided by the department.

c. Internships are intended to serve as a learning process. Sponsors shall assume a training role by providing direction and control of interns. Sponsors shall only sponsor interns who in fact and routinely operate from an office which is within a 50-mile distance of the sponsor's place of business and shall not allow interns to operate independently of such direction and control, or require interns to perform activities which do not enhance the intern's qualification for licensure. In order to acquire the training requisite to obtain the Class "C" license, the intern must in fact and on a routine basis be physically under the direction and control of his/her sponsor. "Physically" contemplates in-person contact on a routine basis with the sponsor and is not accomplished by contact solely by telephone, fax or computer.

d. A Class "C", "M", or "MA" licensee may not sponsor more than six (6) interns at the same time. e. A sponsor shall certify completion or termination of an internship to the department within fifteen (15) days of such occurrence. The certification shall be on a form provided by the department.

Company Identification Cards

a. Every licensed investigative agency must furnish to its partners, principal corporate officers, and all licensed employees an identification card with the name and license number of the holder of the card and name and license number of the agency. The identification card must be signed by the individual licensee and a representative of the agency. The identification card must be in the possession of the licensee at all times while engaged in regulated activity.

b. Agency identification cards are issued solely for the purpose of identifying the licensee and his/her employer. The use of the state seal or the terms "State of Florida", "Department of Agriculture and Consumer Services", or "Division of Licensing" are forbidden. Such terms are often misinterpreted as implying the bearer has some official status.

Applying For a License

a. Any person applying for a license must be at least eighteen (18) years of age; be a citizen of the United States or a legal resident of the United States or have been granted authority to work by the U.S. Citizenship and Immigration Services (USCIS); have no disqualifying criminal history; be of good moral character; have no history of mental illness or history of use of illegal drugs or alcoholism, unless evidence is presented showing successful completion of a rehabilitation program, or current mental competency, as appropriate.

b. The applicant must provide the following: name, date of birth, Social Security number, place of birth, residence addresses for the past five (5) years, occupations for the past five (5) years, a statement of all criminal convictions (including dispositions of adjudication withheld), a statement whether he/she has been adjudicated incapacitated or committed to a mental institution, a statement regarding any history of illegal drug use or alcohol abuse, one (1) full-face color photograph, a full set of prints on the division's fingerprint card, a personal inquiry waiver and the appropriate fees. The submission of the Social Security number is mandatory and is requested pursuant to sections 119.071(5)(a)2, 493.6105, 493.6304, and 493.6406, Florida Statutes, for identification purposes, to prevent misidentification, and to facilitate the approval process. Applications are available from the Department of Agriculture and Consumer Services, Division of Licensing, or any regional office. Applications can also be requested online at http://www.mylicensesite.com. Any non-U.S. citizen who applies for a license under Chapter 493 must submit proof of current employment authorization issued by the U.S. Citizenship and Immigration Services (USCIS).

c. An applicant for a Class "CC" Private Investigator Intern license must be sponsored by a Class "C", "M", or "MA" licensee. The sponsor must submit a notice of intent to sponsor for each Class "CC" licensee under his direction or control.

d. A criminal history record check will be performed by the Florida Department of Law Enforcement and the Federal Bureau of Investigation on each applicant to determine if he/she has a disqualifying criminal history.

Cancellation/Inactivation of License

a. In the event the licensee desires to cancel his/her license, he/she shall notify the department in writing and return the license to the department within ten (10) days of the date of cancellation.

b. The department, at the written request of the licensee, may place his/her license in inactive status. A license may remain inactive for a period of three (3) years, at the end of which time it shall automatically be cancelled if the license has not been renewed. If the license expires during the inactive period, the licensee shall be required to pay license fees before the license can be made inactive. No late fees shall apply when a license is in inactive status.

Agency Advertisements require License Number

A licensed agency must include its agency license number in any advertisement in any print medium or directory, and must include its agency license number in any written bid or offer to provide services.

Example: An agency's license number must be included on bids, Yellow Page listings, trade journals, etc.; however, employment advertising does not require the agency license number.

Other Prohibited Acts

a. Impersonating, or permitting or aiding and abetting an employee to impersonate, a law enforcement officer or an employee of the state, the United States, or any political subdivision thereof by identifying himself/herself as a federal, state, county, or municipal law enforcement officer or official representative, by wearing a uniform or presenting or displaying a badge or credentials that would cause a reasonable person to believe that he/she is a law enforcement officer or that he/she has official authority, by displaying any flashing or warning vehicular lights other than amber-colored, or by committing any act that is intended to falsely convey official status.

b. Fraud or willful misrepresentation in applying for or obtaining a license.

c. Use of any fictitious or assumed name by an agency unless the agency has Division of Licensing approval and has registered that name with Department of State, Division of Corporations.

d. Being found guilty of or entering a plea of guilty or *nolo contendere* to, regardless of adjudication, or being convicted of a crime which directly relates to the business for which the license is held or sought. A plea of *nolo contendere* shall create a rebuttable presumption of guilt to the underlying criminal charges, and the department shall allow the individual being disciplined or denied an application for a license to present any mitigating evidence relevant to the reason for, and the circumstances surrounding, his/her plea.

e. A false statement by the licensee that any individual is or has been in his/her employ.

f. A finding that the licensee or any employee is guilty of willful betrayal of a professional secret or any unauthorized release of information acquired as a result of activities regulated under this chapter.

g. Conducting activities regulated under Chapter 493 without a license or with a revoked or suspended license.

h. Proof that the applicant or licensee is guilty of fraud or deceit, or of negligence, incompetence, or misconduct in the practice of the activities regulated under Chapter 493.

Example: It is misconduct to refuse to provide a copy of an investigative report to a client upon demand when such report resulted from investigative activity paid for by the client.

Example: It is deceit in the practice of regulated activities to refuse to provide a client a bill itemizing all charges upon demand by the client.

i. Commission of an act of violence or the use of force on any person except in the lawful protection of one's self or another from physical harm.

j. Knowingly violating, advising, encouraging, or assisting the violation of any statute, court order, capias, warrant, injunction, or cease and desist order, in the course of business regulated under Chapter 493.

k. Soliciting business for an attorney in return for compensation.

l. Transferring or attempting to transfer a license issued pursuant to Chapter 493. *Section 493.6118(1)(m), F.S.* m. Employing or contracting with any unlicensed or improperly licensed person or agency to conduct activities regulated under this chapter when such licensure status was known or could have been ascertained by reasonable inquiry.

n. Failure or refusal to cooperate with or refusal of access to an authorized representative of the department engaged in an official investigation pursuant to Chapter 493.

o. Failure of any partner, principal corporate officer, or licensee to have his/her agency identification card in his/her possession while on duty.

p. Failure of any licensee to have his/her license in his/her possession while on duty, as specified in Section 493.6111(1), F.S. *Section 493.6118(1)(q), F.S.*

q. Failure or refusal by a sponsor to certify completion or termination of an internship to the department within 15 working days. *Section 493.6118(1)(r), F.S.*

r. Failure to report to the department any person whom the licensee knows to be in violation of this chapter or the rules of the department.

s. Violating any provision of Chapter 493.*Section 493.6118(1)(t), F.S.*

t. Felony convictions unless ten (10) years have expired since release from supervision and civil rights have been restored by the state or jurisdiction of conviction.

u. Being found guilty of, entering a plea of guilty to, or entering a plea of *nolo contendere* to a felony and adjudication of guilt is withheld until a period of three (3) years has expired since final release from supervision. *Section 493.6118(4)(c), F.S.*

Use of the State Seal Prohibited

No agency or licensee may use the Great Seal of the State of Florida on any badge, patch, credential, identification card, correspondence, advertisement, business card, or any other means of identification used in connection with investigative services.

Badges

a. Florida law establishes that five-pointed star badges are reserved for wear by sheriffs and deputy sheriffs in this state. Any badge or insignia of such similarity to the official sheriff's badge which is indistinguishable at a distance of twenty (20) feet is prohibited for use by individuals licensed under Chapter 493, F.S.

b. Licensed private investigators and private investigator interns should be especially aware that the use of any badge in the course of investigative activity creates a very strong suggestion of impersonation of a law enforcement officer, an act that would constitute misconduct in the course of regulated activities. ONLY the agency identification card and the Class "C" or "CC" license are needed for identification purposes while on the job. *Sections 30.46, 493.6118(1)(i), and 843.085, F.S.*

Unlawful Symbols of Authority

The unauthorized exhibition, wear or display of any indicia of authority including any badge, insignia, emblem, identification card, uniform or any colorable imitation thereof which could deceive a reasonable person into believing that such item is authorized by a law enforcement agency or the bearer is a law enforcement officer is prohibited. All non-official persons and agencies are prohibited from the use of the words "police", "patrolman", "agent", "sheriff", "deputy", "trooper", "highway patrol", "Wildlife Officer", "Marine Patrol Officer", "state attorney", "public defender", "marshal", "constable", or "bailiff" when the use of such words or combinations thereof could deceive a reasonable person into believing that such person or agency is a law enforcement officer or agency. *Sections 843.085 and 493.6118(1)(i), F.S.*

DOACS Division of Licensing

a. The Department of Agriculture and Consumer Services, Division of Licensing is charged with the duty of regulating the private investigative industry and has authority over both licensed and unlicensed persons and businesses engaged in the field of investigative activity. Such activities are regulated by Chapter 493, Florida Statutes.

b. The department shall have the power to enforce provisions of this chapter, irrespective of the place or location in which the violation occurred, and, upon the complaint of any person or on its own initiative, to cause to be investigated any suspected violation thereof or to cause to be investigated the business and business methods of any licensed or unlicensed person, agency or employee thereof, or applicant for licensure under Chapter 493, F.S.

c. During an investigation by the division, each licensed or unlicensed person, applicant or agency is required by law to provide records and truthfully respond to questions.

d. In the conduct of its enforcement responsibility the division is granted the authority to subpoena any person or records, to take sworn depositions, to issue an order to cease and desist, and to seek injunctive relief from the Circuit Court to assure compliance with the law.

e. Failure or refusal to cooperate with or provide access to an investigator of the division is prohibited by law.

Disciplinary Action/Penalties

a. When the division finds any violations of Chapter 493, it may do one or more of the following:

- Deny an initial or renewal application for license;
- Issue a reprimand;
- Impose an administrative fine up to $1,000 per count or separate offense;
- Place a licensee on probation or suspend or revoke a license.

b. Any person who violates the provisions of Chapter 493 commits a misdemeanor of the first degree.

c. Any person who is convicted of a violation of Chapter 493 is not eligible for licensure for five (5) years.

d. Any person who violates or disregards any cease and desist order issued by the department commits a misdemeanor of the first degree, punishable as provided in Section 775.082 or 775.083, F.S. In addition, the department may seek the imposition of a civil penalty not to exceed $5,000. *Section 493.6120(3), F.S.*

e. Any person who was an owner, officer, partner, or manager of a licensed agency at the time of any activity that is the basis for revocation of the agency or branch office license and who knew or should have known of the activity shall have his/her personal licenses or approval suspended for three (3) years and may not have any financial interest in or be employed in any capacity by a licensed agency during the period of suspension.

Confidentiality

The residence telephone number and residence address of any Class "C", Class "CC", Class "E", or Class "EE" licensee maintained by the department is confidential and exempt from the provisions of Section 119.071(4)(d), F.S., except that the department may provide this information to local, state, or federal law enforcement agencies. When the residence telephone number or residence address of such licensee is, or appears to be, the business telephone number or business address, this information shall be public record.

Divulging Investigative Information

a. Except as otherwise provided by this chapter or other law, no licensee or any employee of a licensee or licensed agency shall divulge or release to anyone other than his/her client or employer the contents of an investigative file acquired in the course of licensed investigative activity. However, the prohibition of this section shall not apply when the client for whom the information was acquired, or his/her lawful representative, has alleged a violation of this chapter by the licensee, licensed agency, or any employee, or when the prior written consent of the client to divulge or release such information has been obtained.

b. Nothing in this section shall be construed to deny access to any business or operational records, except as specified above, by an authorized representative of the department engaged in an official investigation, inspection, or inquiry pursuant to the regulatory duty and investigative authority of this chapter.

c. Any licensee or employee of a licensee or licensed agency who, in reliance on section (a) above, denies access to an investigative file to an authorized representative of the department shall state such denial in writing within two (2) working days of the request for access. Such statement of denial shall include the following:

1. That the information requested was obtained by a licensed private investigator on behalf of a client; and
2. That the client has been advised of the request and has denied permission to grant access; or

3. That the present whereabouts of the client is unknown or attempts to contact the client have been unsuccessful but, in the opinion of the person denying access, review of the investigative file under conditions specified by the department would be contrary to the interests of the client; or

4. That the requested investigative file will be provided pursuant to a subpoena issued by the department.

d. No licensee or any employer or employee of a licensee or licensed agency shall willfully make a false statement or report to his/her client or employer or to an authorized representative of the department concerning information acquired in the course of activities regulated by this chapter.

Any comments or suggestions regarding this handbook
may be submitted to:

Director
Division of Licensing
Post Office Box 9100
Tallahassee, Florida 32315-9100
Internet Address: http://www.mylicensesite.com
For questions or inquires regarding applications, the application process, or the status of an application or license, please contact:
Division of Licensing Bureau of License Issuance
Post Office Box 9100
Tallahassee, Florida 32315-9100
(850) 245-5691 – Fax (850) 245-5655

You may also contact the regional office in your area:

Fort Walton Regional Office
212 Eglin Parkway S.E., Suite A
Fort Walton Beach, Florida 32548
(850) 833-9146 – Fax (850) 833-9149

Jacksonville Regional Office
7825 Baymeadows Way
Suite 106A, Center Building
Jacksonville, Florida 32256
(904) 448-4341 – Fax (904) 448-4345

Miami Regional Office
401 N.W. Second Avenue, Suite 720-N
Miami, Florida 33128
(305) 377-5950 – Fax (305) 377-5129

Tallahassee Regional Office
1851 N Martin Luther King Jr Boulevard
Tallahassee, Florida 32303
(850) 245-5498 – Fax (850) 414-6159

Orlando Regional Office
1707 Orlando Central Parkway, Suite 150/175
Orlando, Florida 32809
(407) 888-8700

Punta Gorda Regional Office
230 Bal Harbor Boulevard, Suite 111

Punta Gorda, Florida 33950
(941) 575-5770 – Fax (941) 575-5775

Tampa Regional Office
1313 Tampa Street, Suite 712
Tampa, Florida 33602
(813) 272 2552 – Fax (813) 272-2252

West Palm Beach Regional Office
The Forum, Tower A, Suite 100
1675 Palm Beach Lakes Boulevard
West Palm Beach, Florida 33401
(561) 640-6144 – Fax (561) 640-6149
For Walk-In Service Only

Chapter Two
Intern/Sponsorship Relationship

- I. Responsibilities with the sponsorship of interns 493.6116
- II. Letter of intent to sponsor 493.6116 (2) F.S.
- III. Termination/completion of sponsorship 493.6116 (5) F.S.
- IV. Intern semi-annual progress report 493.6116 (5) F
- V. Employee Action Report and its relationship among interns, sponsors, and licensed private investigation agencies.
- VI. Understand the concept of "direction and control" of interns by their sponsors.
- VII. Know the definition of "subcontractor" as defined by the Internal Revenue Service.
- VIII. Understand the prohibitions under Chapter 493, Florida Statute as it relates to being paid for services rendered.

2. Responsibilities of the Sponsorship of Interns

493.6116 Sponsorship of interns.-

(1) Only licensees may sponsor interns. A Class "C," Class "M" or Class "MA" licensee may sponsor a Class "CC" private investigator intern; a Class "E" or Class "MR' licensee may sponsor a Class "EE' recovery agent intern.

(2) M internship may not commence until the sponsor has submitted to the department the notice of intent to sponsor. Such notice shall be on a form provided by the department.

(3) Internship is intended to serve as a learning process. Sponsors shall assume a training status by providing **direction and control of interns**. Sponsors shall only sponsor interns whose place of business is within a 50-mile distance of the sponsor's place of business and shall not allow interns to operate independently of such direction and control, or require interns to perform activities which do not enhance the intern's qualification for licensure.

(4) No sponsor may sponsor more than six interns at the same time.

(5) A sponsor shall certify a biannual progress report on each intern and shall **certify completion or termination** of an internship to the department within 15 days after such completion or termination. The report must be made on a form provided by the department and must include at a minimum:

(a) The inclusive dates of the internship.

(b) A narrative part explaining the primary duties, types of experiences gained, and the scope of training received.

(c) An evaluation of the performance of the intern and a recommendation regarding future licensure.

Independent Contractor

A subcontractor or independent contractor is a person or a company hired by another entity to perform part of the work of a job. For example, an Agency might have an abundance of work and their staff investigators are unable to meet the demand of the extra work. Subcontractors may be hired to handle the "over flow of work". This generally happens in certain busy seasons or with an agency experiencing rapid growth. It could also be the result of a seasonal anomaly or events such as a hurricane that causes an enormous amount of property damage that needs to be inspected and or investigated. Or the ending of a growing season when the migrant workers are no longer needed in the area or when a large plant is closing down and there is a rash of layoffs followed by claims of personal injuries from the workers uncertain about their futures.

Or it can be just a small agency that doesn't have the knowledge or administrative staff or business experience to understand the whole picture.

Often, a freelance investigator will work on a regular basis for several different agencies. The Agency does not employ the investigator as a regular employee in most cases because he/she is not needed on a permanent basis.

493 specifically states that only "A" Agencies can subcontract work from other "A" Agencies. Therefore, if you find that you are working for another agency in an overflow capacity, your main Agency should still be paying you as an employee.

Many Class C investigators hold themselves out to do contract work, however they MUST be employees or part time employees of any Agency they work for as they cannot legally be defined as independent contractors if they don't have a business license per F.S 493 and furthermore they most likely WILL NOT satisfy an IRS audit. So why do so many companies take on subcontractors?

Employee vs. Subcontractor Issues

It has been estimated that hiring an employee costs at least 25 percent more than hiring a subcontractor to perform the same work. You have to match the employee's Social Security and Medicare tax, pay for workers' compensation insurance, liability insurance, provide benefits, and the list goes on. A lot of red tape and a lot of additional cost goes out the window when the "employee" can be classified as a contractor.

Many businesses have attempted to classify workers as independent contractors when they were, in fact, employees. Many businesses have been put **out of business** by the Internal Revenue Service for doing so. If you make this misclassification and the IRS audits you, they will perform the re-class to employee and recalculate the taxes you should have withheld, calculate interest and penalties, possibly hit you and any other responsible party with the 100 percent penalty, and bill you for all of the above. It won't matter if the contractor paid the taxes or not. If they did, you will have to find them and prove that they did in order to receive credit for taxes they paid. The IRS will assume that the contractor/employees paid none of their taxes. The end result of such a reclassification is usually more than a business can bear and you can expect **absolutely no mercy**!

You may also run into similar problems if the contractor is hurt on the job and wants to collect workers' compensation or if he gets sued for damages and either doesn't have his own liability insurance or is underinsured. I think you get the picture. It can get plenty ugly!

The IRS has developed a list of 20 factors it uses to test employee or subcontractor status. The Department of Labor and state boards will normally follow these as well. Here are the twenty factors you should be aware of before deciding to call an employee an independent contractor.

1. Does the business require the worker to follow their instructions on how work is to be performed? If yes, this indicates employee status. An independent contractor will generally decide how the project should be completed and use his own methodology.

2. Does the business provide training to the worker? If you're hiring a person for a job they are not trained for and providing them with the training to carry it out, that person is probably an employee. There can be exceptions based on the facts and circumstances, but if you fail this test, you might lose no matter how many of the others you pass.

3. Are the worker's services a substantial or integral part of the business? This indicates employee status because it indicates the business maintains direction and control over the worker.

4. Does the business require the worker to perform all services personally? Independent contractors may have their own employees or at least should have the option of hiring other contractors to perform their work. Agreements for personal services indicate employee status.

5. Does the business hire, supervise and pay the worker's assistants? If so, this is a strong indication of employee status. Let the independent contractor pay his or her own assistants.

6. Does the business have an ongoing relationship with the worker? This one is a stretch since many businesses maintain lifelong relationships with

contractors whose work they like. But the IRS views this as an indication of employee status.

7. Does the business set the worker's schedule and hours? Independent contractors generally set their own work schedules. If the contractor must work certain hours because of required interrelationships with your employees or to take advantage of down time for computer-related work, document these facts.

8. Does the business require the worker full-time? This is an indication of employee status because the business controls their availability and prevents them from working on other clients.

9. Does the business provide the workspace? Contractors who work off-site are more likely to be classified an independent contractor.

10. Does the business determine the order or sequence in which work is completed? Indicates employee status. If specific schedules are required, document them in the contract with the reasoning for doing so.

11. Does the business require oral or written reports? The IRS believes regular written or oral reports detailing the work completed indicates employee status. In reality, this is, and should be, expected from independent contractors as well.

12. Does the business pay by the hour, week or month? This indicates employee status.

13. Does the business pay expenses? This is an indication that the business is directing the Independent contractor's business activities. Make sure the independent contractor pays the expenses and bills you for reimbursement.

14. Does the business provide tools and equipment for the worker? Independent contractors would normally provide their own tools and equipment.

15. Does the worker have a significant investment in their own facilities? If the contractor maintains his own office space, computer equipment, tools, etc., this is a good indication that they are an independent contractor.

16. Does the worker have profits and losses independent of the business? This is an indication that the contractor is running his own bona fide business and is an independent contractor.

17. Does the worker have multiple clients? Working with multiple clients generally indicates independent contractor status.

18. Does the worker market their services to the general public? Employees do not generally market their services to the general public.

19. Does the business have the right to discharge the worker at any time? This suggests employee status. An independent contractor would only be discharged for failure to meet contract specifications.
20. Does the worker have the right to quit at any time? An independent contractor is under contract and cannot quit until the project is completed.

The purpose of these factors is to attempt to determine whether the employer has the right to control the worker, how, when and where the work is performed, and the amount of investment the worker has in his own business. The higher degree of control the employer has over the worker, the more likely the IRS will classify the worker as an employee. As you can see, there is a high degree of subjectivity in these tests. Some consultants will tell you that you're in danger if your worker falls into the employee category on more than 7 to 9 of these guidelines. I can tell you from experience that you may be in trouble if you fail on only **three or four!** The test **is** highly subjective and an IRS agent may feel strongly that the requisite control is evidenced even if you pass most of the guidelines with flying colors.

The entire point of looking at these guidelines and applying them to your particular facts and circumstances is to determine if classification as an independent contractor is worth the risk and, if you decide that it is, to determine how to shore up your position before the work begins. At a minimum you should do each of the following to make sure your case is as strong as it can be.

1. Put your agreement with the independent contractor in writing. Include a description of the project, the expected duration, the amount to be paid and how it is to be paid, a paragraph specifically acknowledging that the worker is an independent contractor, and as many other details as can be agreed on. Specify that the worker must supply his own insurances. Ask for the insurance certificates and keep them on file.
2. Get a completed I-9 form from the worker and be prepared to issue a 1099 at year's end.
3. Save any promotional materials, proposals, etc. that the contractor has given you. Also save the promotional materials, proposals, etc. that you got from other contractors competing for your work. Document why you selected this contractor.
4. Pay only on invoices submitted to you by the contractor. Even if the contract is for an hourly rate, let the contractor maintain the records of hours worked and bill you for them. You may, of course, keep your own records to verify this.
5. If at all possible, do not pay on an hourly basis. You may have to, but if possible break down the amounts to be paid based on deliverables throughout the life of the project. You may pay periodic draws to aid the contractor's cash flow, but make sure the contractor accounts for them on his bills as draws against his billing for the deliverables.

6. If the project runs over the original budget and the original contract terms, address this issue in writing. If you're prepared to pay the extra fees, add a contract addendum to cover it. If the project scope changes and you require additional work, add a contract addendum for that as well.

Even with the above documentation there is no guarantee that you will prevail if the IRS comes knocking. But without such documentation, you may be risking your business!

Chapter Three
Professional Ethics

    I.   Understand the client/investigator relationship
    II.   Recognize the importance of the initial client interview
    III.   Understand Whether a Client's Intentions are Legal and Ethical
    IV.   Establish a Clear Understanding of Clients Goals
    V.   Working a Case in a Timely and Cost Effective Manner
    VI.   Provide Regular Updates and Reports
    VII.   Confidentiality
    VIII. Potential Conflicts of Interest
    IX.   Providing a Quality Work Product
    X.   Providing Detailed Reports and Invoices
    XI.   Truth in Advertising
    XII.   Agency to Agency Billing

3. Understand the Client/Investigator Relationship.

According to 493, your relationship with your client and your assignment is confidential and no one other than your client should be privileged to your investigation or the result thereof. You cannot go into a neighborhood and say, "I'm investigating Joe Neighbor, tell me what you know about him". You must be discreet and always remember entering and exiting a neighborhood without anyone even knowing you where there is always the prime principle of your investigation.

I always approach a case thinking that blending in is the most important tactic to getting people to willingly provide information. I have heard of instances where the police or an over bearing PI tries to use his credentials to get information and the witness says I am busy, doesn't want to get involved or simply states they don't know anything and the investigator walks away without any information. Conversely, a smooth talking friendly PI who approaches the house under the pre-text that he is thinking about moving into the neighborhood may have a better chance. I have had woman at the door tell me to hold on while she reduces the heat to her stove burner and invites me into the house for a cup of tea and talk about where I am from and what brings me to the community. This may be the same woman that told the obtrusive investigator that she didn't know anything and was busy cooking dinner. Your approach to gathering information and how you handle people is crucial!

Recognize the Importance of the Initial Client Interview.

During your initial contact with your client make sure you understand exactly what they are looking for and realize they may not address or have all the information you may need. After all they are not the professional investigator and may not know what is important or critical to your investigation. You may need to review the information provided at the initial contact then conduct some preliminary efforts before re-contacting the client with some additional questions. Make sure you have a plan of attack so that the client is confident in their decision to hire you. Don't say, "what would you like me to do or what do you think I should do?" At the same time don't let an overbearing client tell you how to conduct an investigation. You are the professional and should develop a plan of action after reviewing all the information provided by the client.

Client's Intentions- Legal and Ethical?

Just because a client calls you to perform an investigation doesn't mean you don't have a moral and perhaps legal obligation to make certain the clients' intentions are legal and ethical. Exactly why are you being asked to perform a specific service. For what and how is the information going to be used. If it is a locate investigation, then you need to determine why and for what purpose you are locating the subject. You need to consider the possibility that the other subject doesn't want to be found due to domestic violence issues or perhaps even an Order of Protection granted to the other party to keep the client away. When I first started in the business my territory was South Florida and the Keys. I was sitting on a WC surveillance assignment when I noticed a male subject exit a house on the same block I was parked. I was well away from my target house and actually sitting off of them because I knew the subject's schedule having worked it several times before. I was merely sitting down the street a couple of blocks waiting for my subjects car to leave the driveway, when the male subject on my block approached my passenger's side window and places a small firearm at the side of my head. He asked me what I was doing and without hesitation I told him I was doing surveillance. After things calmed down, I immediately called the Hollywood Police Department and reported the incident and requested he be arrested. After my assignment I spend two hours in the PD being talked out of filing charges by the DEA. The subject who had pulled the gun on me was a DEA agent supposedly on leave of absence after an incident in Mexico where his partner was captured, tortured and killed. What I also learned is that Private Investigators where being used by the drug cartels. Unbeknown to local PI's they were being hired by the cartels representing themselves as local businessmen wanting to investigate their business partners. Since the DEA often used undercover locations in unmarked office suites in ordinary strip plazas throughout south Florida, there was no way to know who was actually using the space. The hired investigators were told to go to the business location and take a picture of each subject exiting the office, identify their car when they leave and perhaps even follow them home to identify their address. The investigators were told that once the information was gathered, the client would then take it from to analyze the information. What was thought to be an internal corporate security or business intelligence operation, actually turned out to be intelligence supporting a criminal enterprise. As a young investigator, I quickly realized the complexity of my current issue with the DEA agent who perhaps over reacting but was in fear of his family who was at home at the time. Not wanting to blemish his years of service, I dropped my charges.

Many states have adopted, a Drivers Privacy Protection Act (DPPA) protecting the privacy of peoples state motor vehicle record information. However in many states this information is still available to the professional investigator, but we need to understand why our clients need this information, because the abuses are real and well known.

In California, the Driver Protection Act DPPA was passed in reaction to a series of abuses of drivers' personal information held by the DMV and other government bodies. The 1989 death of actress Rebecca Schaeffer was a prominent example of such abuse. In that case, a private investigator, hired by an obsessed fan, was able to obtain Rebecca Schaeffer's address through her California motor vehicle record. The fan used her address information to stalk and to kill her. Other incidents around the US and cited by Congress included a ring of Iowa home robbers who targeted victims by writing down the license plates of expensive cars and obtaining home address information from the State's department of motor vehicles.

Senator Barbara Boxer, of California who sponsored 103 S. 1589, a version of the DPPA, cited other examples where stalkers were able to find victims by simply visiting a DMV. She argued that in 34 States, someone could walk into a State Motor Vehicle Department with your license plate number and a few dollars and walk out with your name and home address." Senator Boxer also said:

"In Tempe, AZ, a woman was murdered by a man who had obtained her home address from that State's DMV.

And, in California, a 31-year-old man copied down the license plate numbers of five women in their early twenties, obtained their home address from the DMV and then sent them threatening letters at home. I want to briefly read from two of those letters.

I'm lonely and so I thought of you. I'll give you one week to respond or I will come looking for you.

Another one read: *I looked for you though all I knew about you was your license plate. Now I know more and yet nothing. I know you're a Libra, but I don't know what it's like to smell your hair while I'm kissing your neck and holding you in my arms.*

When they apprehended this subject, they found in his possession a book entitled `You Can Find Anyone' which spelled out how to do just that using someone's license plate.

Americans are in favor of laws protecting their personal information and privacy. Without these laws Americans are not secure in their own homes. It is easy for anyone anywhere to access information as personal as your address and phone number, even if they are not listed in the telephone directory. Even your Social Security number is available. Many Americans are infuriated and, more importantly, they are vulnerable to these violations of privacy.

Recently, a woman in Virginia was shocked to discover black balloons and antiabortion literature on her doorstep days after she had visited a health clinic that performs abortions. Apparently, someone used her license plate number to track down personal information which was used to stalk her.

In another case in Georgia, an obsessive fan obtained the home address of a fashion model from the State Department of Motor Vehicles and assaulted her in front of her apartment.

These are just a few examples of how information gathered can if in the wrong hands be misused. As Professional Investigators, we need to understand that our privileged access to information sometimes restricted to others can be used to harm others if the intent is not clearly understood.

Protect Yourself; Establish The Client's Goals and Contract.

Make sure you ask for what is the information going to be used and have the purpose clearly defined in a written contract between you and the client. Indicate on your contract that the information may not be used or disseminated to a third party or for any reason not stipulated in the contract.

Timely and Cost-Effective Procedures

Competition today is brutal as more and more investigators offer services. Clients expect a swift turnaround time with a case usually handled within three days of the assignment and a full written report within a weeks time. Clients also want to know up front what the case will cost them. I try to Flat Rate my charges so the client knows exactly what my services will cost them. This is a pretty accepted practice if you think about it. Most industries do the same thing, an oil change $35.00 and brake job $199.00. These industries have refined their services and know the amount of time each task takes. You should do the same thing, people are put off by investigators that ask for large retainers or can't tell the client what the case will cost. Learn to break up or package your services so they are affordable. Offer a Flat Rate day of surveillance which includes all travel time, mileage and expenses. The going rate in 2012 is around $550.00 a day. For Domestic Cases you may charge less or reduce the amount of time you spend per day on a file. A flat rate of $250.00 is manageable and should get you business. For Domestic cases packages you will need to shorten your day to keep the costs down and utilize the spouse to set up a *sting operation*.

Provide Regular Updates and Reports.

Like any profession communication is important to stay on the same page as your client so that there is a clear understanding of what is expected and what has been promised. Results can not be promised but with a solid plan they are usually produced. Give your client regular updates and follow-up your investigation with a full written report and invoice. The target turnaround time to complete an investigation and submit your written report should be two weeks.

Confidentiality.

Clients don't always understand the legalities of matters so explaining them is important. Your work is confidential but then the work you generate may be sensitive as well and must be handled accordingly.

Dissemination of Information.

The product you create should be turned over to your client. If it is sensitive then indicate so. Criminal and other background records may reflect information not readily available to the public. You would not want a disgruntled worker hiring you so he could spread damaging information around the office about the subject. Divorce cases can be equally ugly with child custody battles and reputation wars. One says things about the other, but when a Professional Investigator is hired, the innuendoes become searchable facts if developed are reported on with ample evidence and corroborative support. However used outside the courtroom for more sinister reasons may violate your dissemination guideline or even damage your adverse parties' reputation and become libelous. Let your client know the criminal record you provided is to be used for court not copied and sent to his boss or co-workers at the office. Making sure you have a clear dissemination policy and understanding with your client will keep you out of trouble.

Identify Potential Conflicts of Interests.

When we chose a specialty we also in some cases choose a side. If you work Insurance defense you can't also work for a personal Injury Attorney. Imagine being the investigator that was given a surveillance assignment then asked by the a plaintiffs attorney firm to video "a day in the life of the claimant", something plaintiff attorneys like to do to show the difficulties the plaintiff lives with on a daily basis. Obviously the investigator would be providing conflicting documentation. We wouldn't also want to represent both a husband and a wife

Provide a Quality Work Product.

Well, let me put it to you this way, your name goes on the bottom of the report. As with any business, the cream rises to the top and you are only as good as your last report. Building a reputation in a highly competitive industry is only possible through sustained and maintained quality. You can maintain a business working for different people all of the time but maintaining a corporate client requires hard work and diligent efforts. Substandard work has no place in our industry but unfortunately it exits and a lot of it. I am embarrassed sometimes when I read or review an investigation that was referred to me. My only solitude is that the client recognized the poor quality and lack of results and has sought out a different vendor and now I have the opportunity to satisfy another client and continued to build my client base. Longevity in the industry can only come about through maintaining high business standards and wanting to deliver results to your client. Sometime this takes more time than authorized, but if you're committed to getting results you're not counting hours you're gauging your progress. My dad use to say, my time is worth nothing, focus on your product and everything else will fall in place. Lets face it this is not a cookie cutter job; you never know what you may have to do get the job done so stay flexible. Your effort is only limited by your imagination.

Detailed Reports and Invoices

It may be hard for you to justify your bill or explain in detail what information you uncovered or the efforts that went into the case if you can't write a detailed report. Typically a report may have a synopsis or conclusion that can relay facts quickly, but in a courtroom setting, you must have detailed notes that are transcribed in report form and show your efforts in chronological order by date and time. Your invoice also needs to look professional and should contain your EIN, address and of course a detailed account of your billing, usually by day if you use the flat rate system. The invoice should also contain a notice to the client that they have 30 days to pay or payment due upon receipt and then a [penalty of an interest for late payments. I give my corporate clients 30 days to pay but then add a penalty of 2% per month if not paid on time.

Truth in Advertising

We have all heard the terms of bait and switch in which a client is offered one thing then given something completely different. When you are first starting a business or entering the world of entrepreneurship, you suddenly realize there is more to running a business than just conducting great investigations. Most State Agencies will not permit superlative like "The Best PI Firm in the County", because it is difficult backup a claim like that. Simply put the Federal Trade Commission specifically outlines three basic rules which it applies in determining if an advertisement is truthful or in violation of the set standards for Truth in Advertising". These rules are as follows:

- Advertising must be truthful and non-deceptive;
- Advertisers must have evidence to back up their claims; and
- Advertisements cannot be unfair.

What makes an advertisement deceptive?

According to the FTC's Deception Policy Statement, an ad is deceptive if it contains a statement - or omits information – that is likely to mislead consumers acting reasonably under the circumstances; and is "material" - that is, important to a consumer's decision to buy or use the product.

What makes an advertisement unfair?

According to the Federal Trade Commission Act and the FTC's Unfairness Policy Statement, an ad or business practice is unfair if it causes or is likely to cause substantial consumer injury which a consumer could not reasonably avoid; and it is not outweighed by the benefit to consumers.

How does the FTC determine if an ad is deceptive?

The FTC looks at the ad from the point of view of the "reasonable consumer" - the typical person looking at the ad. Rather than focusing on certain words, the FTC looks at the ad in context - words, phrases, and pictures - to determine what it conveys to consumers.

The FTC looks at both "express" and "implied" claims. An express claim is literally made in the ad. For example, "ABC Mouthwash prevents colds" is an express claim that the product will prevent colds. An implied claim is one made indirectly or by inference. "ABC Mouthwash kills the germs that cause colds" contains an implied claim that the product will prevent colds. Although the ad doesn't literally say that the product prevents colds, it would be reasonable for a consumer to conclude from the statement "kills the germs that cause colds" that the product will prevent colds. Under the law, advertisers must have proof to back up express and implied claims that consumers take from an ad.

The FTC looks at what the ad does not say - that is, if the failure to include information leaves consumers with a misimpression about the product. For example, if a company advertised a collection of books, the ad would be deceptive if it did not disclose that consumers actually would receive abridged versions of the books.

The FTC looks at whether the claim would be "material" - that is, important to a consumer's decision to buy or use the product. Examples of material claims are representations about a product's performance, features, safety, price, or effectiveness.

The FTC looks at whether the advertiser has sufficient evidence to support the claims in the ad. The law requires that advertisers have proof before the ad runs. What kind of evidence must a company have to support the claims in its ads?
Before a company runs an ad, it has to have a "reasonable basis" for the claims. A "reasonable basis" means objective evidence that supports the claim. The kind of evidence depends on the claim. At a minimum, an advertiser must have the level of evidence that it says it has. For example, the statement "Two out of three doctors recommend ABC Pain Reliever" must be supported by a reliable survey to that effect. If the ad isn't specific, the FTC looks at several factors to determine what level of proof is necessary including what experts in the field think is needed to support the claim. In most cases, ads that make health or safety claims must be supported by "competent and reliable scientific evidence" - tests, studies, or other scientific evidence that has been evaluated by people qualified to review it. In addition, any tests or studies must be conducted using methods that experts in the field accept as accurate.

Are letters from satisfied customers sufficient to substantiate a claim? No. Statements from satisfied customers usually are not sufficient to support a health or safety claim or any other claim that requires objective evaluation.

My company offers a money-back guarantee. Very few people have ever asked for their money back. Must we still have proof to support our advertising claims? Yes. Offering a money-back guarantee is not a substitute for substantiation. Advertisers still must have proof to support their claims.

What penalties can be imposed against a company that runs a false or deceptive ad?

The penalties depend on the nature of the violation. The remedies that the FTC or the courts have imposed include: Cease and desist orders. These legally-binding orders require companies to stop running the deceptive ad or engaging in the deceptive practice, to have substantiation for claims in future ads, to report periodically to FTC staff about the substantiation they have for claims in new ads, and to pay a fine of $16,000 per day per ad if the company violates the law in the future. Civil penalties range from thousands of dollars to millions of dollars, depending on the nature of the violation. Sometimes advertisers have been ordered to give full or partial refunds to all consumers who bought the product.

Advertisers have been required to take out new ads to correct the misinformation conveyed in the original ad, notify purchasers about deceptive claims in ads, include specific disclosures in future ads, or provide other information to consumers.

Agency-to-Agency billing.

Only an "A Agency" can advertise for business. Typically when one agency calls another for assistance, they are looking for assistance at a discounted rate. If the agency charges $75.00 hour then typically will offer their investigators out for around $50.00 an hour. This usually takes place among smaller sized agencies that need to share workers to cover a greater territory. In today's market with so many Nationwide Agencies, companies that can't cover an entire state are consider almost too small to compete and retain large business accounts. So having a good network of agencies that will offer you a discounted rate so you can still profit on your client relationship is a very important element to running a successful business. The discounted rate is important to the business owner and referring agency because they will also have to supervise the referral as well as make sure the report is prepared to the referring companies standards. The reports either done in house or through subcontracted agency, still needs to look the same as the referring companies normal product they deliver everyday. This takes time which is paid for through the up charge of the referring agency normal billable rate. For example, a case referred to another agency for an eight hour surveillance will cost $50.00 X 8 or $400.00. Based on the average charge of $550.00 per day this leaves $150.00 for the referring agencies bottom time and effort.

Chapter Four
Legal Issues in Investigations

I. Introduction
II. Law enforcement notification requirement.
III. Invasion of Privacy
IIV. Legal Parameters of Trespassing.
V. Falsification of Information in Reports
VI. Misrepresentation of Authority.
VII. Proper Release of Information.
VIII. Chain of Custody Procedure

4. Introduction

When surveillance was first introduced to the corporate business environment it raised concern to those that felt it could affect or hurt their cases. In particular Personal Injury attorneys saw this rising technique by insurance companies as an invasion of their client's privacy. They went as far to threaten Insurance companies that its use would cause intentional infliction of emotional distress of their clients. Soon letters threatening the above started going out to many large insurance carriers. Since the letters were suspiciously similar it was apparent that the statewide plaintiffs' bar organization conceived this scheme to frighten insurers away from using surveillance.

This prompted immediate research and study of case law to make sure surveillance was available option. Many large Private Investigations firms hired attorneys to investigate the law. At that time, I was a rising manager in one of these firms and we too took on the matter so as to defend our future business plans.

Simply put, our research indicated that reasonable surveillance activities do not give rise to causes of actions for invasion of privacy or intentional infliction of emotional distress by plaintiffs.

There are other concerns as well the Private Investigator must be aware of. This chapter will address some of the Criminal and Civil Liabilities we are faced with.

Law Enforcement Notification

When you are conducting a surveillance in a community it is a courtesy to notify the local law enforcement officers by checking in with dispatch upon arriving on the scene and providing your specific location. You are to also to provide your vehicle tag number, type and color of vehicle, your name, and your company name and telephone number.

There are some grey areas to this rule as you will find that not all municipalities reciprocate the hospitality. In fact I have been in Counties in which the Sheriff has told me he does not allow surveillance in "his" county. So in this case, you could understand why I didn't want to check in and why I made darn sure no one ever knew I was there when I came to work. So things are not always as cut and dry as they seem. Moreover, although we are encouraged to check in, if you ask nay dispatch officer okay, now that I have checked in, what is your policy for handling calls in reference to my vehicle? You will find that they do not have any policy as their loyalty is always to their community. They simply state, He is a Private Investigator. So given this scenario, what is the motivation for us to call in? They say it is to stop officers from coming to our location and blowing our under cover effort. But we are parked far enough away from our subjects to avoid this and if we are doing what we are supposed to do; chances are no one even knows we are there. As you will find and hear many times over in this course, a good investigator is to enter and exit the area without anyone every knowing her/she was there.

Finally, I will relate one other issue that you must take into consideration when you are considering checking in. Many people in small towns listen to police scanners and when they hear, "Sgt. Bob, this is control, I just wanted to let you know we just had a Private investigator check in at the corner of Main and Fifth" The next thing you know the who neighborhood knows you are there and you might not of done anything wrong.

The Right of Privacy

The right of privacy actually consists of a number of separate but related rights arising from a variety of legal sources.

A constitutional right of privacy has been found in the U.S. Constitution. This right is currently the subject of much debate because of the nationwide controversy over abortion. Article I, 23, of the Florida Constitution expressly recognizes a right of privacy. The right of privacy under both constitutions protects the individual against governmental intrusions into privacy, but not against intrusions by private individuals or businesses.

Florida and most other states recognize a common-law right of privacy. In some instances, this common law right of privacy has been incorporated into statues and governmental regulations, some of which have enlarged its scope. If plaintiffs do possess a tort cause of action for invasion of privacy resulting from an insurer's surveillance activities, it will be found in the common law right or privacy.

Essentially, the common law right of privacy is the right to be let alone and to live in a community without being held up to the public gaze against one's will. The common law tort actually consists of four distinct privacy interests, which, if invaded, give rise to four distant but related causes of action. These causes of action are called appropriation, intrusion of true privacy, public disclosure or private facts, and false light in the public eye.

Appropriation occurs when the defendant appropriates a person's name or likeness for defendant's commercial advantage. Intrusion of true privacy occurs when the defendant invades plaintiff's private affairs or seclusion in a way that would be objectionable to a reasonable person. The intrusion must be into something that is private – taking pictures of someone in a public place is not actionable. Public disclosure of private facts occurs when the defendant publishes private information about the plaintiff that would be objectionable to a person of ordinary sensibilities. Finally, the tort of false light in the public eye occurs when the defendant publishes facts about the plaintiff, which place the plaintiff in a false light in the public eye. The false light must be something that is objectionable to a person or ordinary sensibilities.

Surveillance and Privacy

Generally, one who seeks to recover damages from another must expect that his claim will be investigated and, therefore, waives his right of privacy to the extent of a reasonable investigation. Because of the public interest in exposing fraudulent claims, reasonable investigation and surveillance of a claimant's activities to determine the validity of a claim are generally not held to be tortuous. Thus, defendants have the right to investigate any and all claims which may have been filed against them and to make such investigation, as they deem necessary.

Similarly, it has been held that insurance companies have the right to investigate any and all possible claims which might be filed against them or their insured's. If the surveillance is conducted in a reasonable and unobtrusive manner, the insurer will incur no liability for invasion of privacy. However, if the investigation is conducted in an unreasonable and obtrusive manner, a defendant may be liable for invasion of privacy. A Georgia court has held, for instance, that a defendant does not have the right to make an investigation in a conspicuous manner sufficient to excite the speculation of the plaintiff's neighbors. An Alabama court has held that there may be an actionable violation of the right to privacy where the person is watched, trailed, shadowed or kept under surveillance in an offensive or improper manner.

Generally, however, courts have upheld a defendant's right to conduct reasonable investigation and surveillance. Thus, in one Florida case where the investigator accidentally exposed himself while trailing the plaintiff on a public highway while trying to investigate the validity of her personal injury claim, the court held that the investigator was not liable for invasion of privacy in the absence of facts showing that the surveillance was intended to harass or intimidate her into involuntary settlement.

A Pennsylvania court held that surveillance films of the plaintiff did not constitute invasion of privacy. The films did not contain embarrassing pictures of the plaintiff, and the sole purpose of the film was to record the plaintiff's movements and daily activities. The court noted that if the films disclosed inconsistencies in the plaintiff's claim "any embarrassment suffered by her would be justified."

Legal Guidelines for Surveillants

The basic legal principles on which surveillants operate are those that do not violate an individual's constitutional rights. There are some principles that serve as general guidelines in this area.

A subject in public view cannot successfully contend that his actions are secret, or that any surveillance of those actions constitutes an invasion of his privacy. Privacy pertains to places where the subject has a "reasonable expectation of privacy", (such as behind a stockade fence), not to public places or movement. To view and observe a subject traveling a public thoroughfare, on a public street, in a public or commercial building, on a golf course, in a public transit vehicle or even in his own garden or public business place would not violate his right to privacy.

Once a subject has entered a private building and the "curtains are drawn" and no easy view is presented to the outside public, and no view of him can be had without using a "Peeping Tom" type of surveillance, then it could be an invasion of privacy.

The courts have recognized the use of optical aids for the extension of human vision in physical surveillance, such as binoculars and telescopes, and admitted the evidential value of photographic evidence, and thus the use of still and video camera equipped with telephoto or zoom lenses. Use of such aids is not considered a violation of the subject's Fourth Amendment rights. Minnesota court, for example, held that the defendant's claim that the "use of a telescopic device" was a form of "unreasonable search" was "without merit". In another case, the court said, "the use of binoculars did not change the character or admissibility of evidence or information gained". If, however, optical aids were used to peer into a subject's home, the courts would tend to rule that this violated the intent of the Fourth Amendment. The use of photographic evidence has long been accepted in courts of the land, and therefore, the equipment that produces such evidence is recognized as a legal aid in investigation.

Each investigator should have on his person a copy of the statues governing Private Investigators. In Florida this would be Florida Statutes 493.6100. This statue states that investigators are authorized under Florida Statutes 493 to conduct surveillances and investigation anywhere in Florida with reference to any matter or any person, including the following:

"The identity, conduct, movements, affiliations, association, transactions, reputation or character or any person or group or persons".

Be further advised that Florida Statues 493.6119 (1) reads as follows:

"No licensee or employee of any licensee shall divulge or relate to any person other than his principal or his employer any information acquired as the result of any surveillance in investigation".

"Any person violating this section is guilty of a first degree misdemeanor, punishable by Statute 775.082 or Statute 775.083.

Most of the states we are currently licensed in have compatible statues.

Trespassing

When "No Trespassing" signs are posted this is your initial warning and should you be caught violating or trespassing you will be cited or arrested.

If the area is no posting, you are entitled to ONE warning.

Most private properties such as apartment complexes, condominiums, private clubs, and golf courses have signs posted stating this is private property. They may not state no trespassing however and you are entitled to one warning or request to leave the premises. After this warning is given you should immediately leave and figure out another way to perform your investigation.

On the other hand a grumpy neighbor cannot ask you to leave his neighborhood or move your car away form his house if you are parked on the side of a public roadway. A public roadway is any paved or concrete roadway that is maintained by the state or local government.

Trespassing is usually not a problem or an issue if you use good judgment. I can say that in my 30 years as a PI, I have never been trespassed, cited or arrested for trespass (knock on wood).

But be aggressive, the worst thing to hear from an investigator is that he couldn't get video because of the area or was afraid to enter the woods, man-up! What you may be too timid to do, another competitor will and you'll lose a client.

Falsification of Reports

Simply put, our investigations are used in legal proceedings that effect peoples lives. Falsifying a report is not only a crime it will get you stripped of your license to be a private investigator and livelihood. In the industry, "Ghosting" is when a person makes up parts of a report usually during surveillance because they weren't there. For example, the investigator is to start his surveillance at 6:00 a.m., but he never gets there until 9:00 a.m., yet in his report he writes he got there at 6:00 a.m. and proceeds to state what he saw. This is usually done when the investigator has worked the case before and knows the persons vehicles or pattern of activity and upon arriving notices the vehicles present so figures or reports no activity took place up until the time he actually arrived. I had an employee once who never shot any film in the mornings and when he did finally shoot some film, he usually then just immediately left. I started to get the impression he was not getting to his surveillances on time in the morning and then when he did arrive if he shot some film of the subject getting the mail or running to the store, he would then just leave. This was not what he was being paid for. He was being paid to conduct eight hours of surveillance usually from 6:00 a.m. – 2:00 p.m.

Based on my hunch that he was 'Ghosting", I assigned him a typical case in Lakeland, Florida, approximately 30 minutes from his house. I then had my assistant manager, go to his house and sit and watch to see what time he left. On that day, the investigator left, but with his wife who he took to the mall where she cut hair. This was at 9:00 a.m., and the investigator got back to the house at 9:30 a.m. The investigator then finally left by himself at 10:12 a.m. having loaded up his camera gear.

I wanted three days for the report on this surveillance to hit my desk and upon reading the report the hours worked read 6:02 a.m. – 2:04 p.m. I had my assistant manager print out the time and date stamped still pictures of his car at the house at 9:00 a.m. and of him entering the vehicle with his wife and then when he returned to the house at 10:12 a.m. I immediately told him he was being fired and to turn in all of his equipment. I subsequently wrote up the matter in detail along with the still pictures, an affidavit from my assistant manager and forwarded the Investigator's report and my investigation to DOACS. A hearing was subsequently held at which time I testified on behalf of the company and as a witness for the state in the revocation of the investigator's license.

No company wants a rogue investigator jeopardizing the reputation of their firm. After all businesses are just groups of people with a common purpose providing a service or product. While the business may be the brain child of one, it supports many other people and their families. No mater how bright and ambitious an entrepreneur may be, he must have good people around him with a common goal. No one should allow such a practice to take place and any direct knowledge or suspicions of ghosting should be immediately reported to your supervisor.

Misrepresentation of Authority

As provided in the statute, misrepresentation of a Court, State, Federal or County employee is expressly prohibited. Moreover misrepresenting yourself as a Police Officer of any type is a Felony.

Investigator must be very careful when using pretexts not to use those that suggest you are a court appointed officer, Police Officer or acting in some other official capacity that would make the civilian think you are an agent of the government on any level. Typically, I say I am an investigator when I really need to get some information, but this is as far as I go. I show them my State Private Investigators License and I don't carry a badge of any sort. Depending on the impression or conclusions they draw that's their own concern. If questioned I state I showed them my ID and again show this same ID to whoever may enquire. The person recalls me showing them my ID and since it states I am a Private Investigator, they are the ones that failed to review the document close enough. In other instances, if I am working an Insurance case, I say I am an Insurance or Claims Investigator.

Proper Release of Information.

The dissemination of information is always a concern to the Professional Investigator. You are developing information for your client and typically it is for their eyes or the courts only. Some of the information is sensitive and may involve criminal records. If we run a FDLE criminal records search, the Criminal History comes to you with a paragraph reading this information is sensitive and should not be disseminated to any "third party". In other words the information was not meant to be photocopied 10 0times and dropped all over town. More specifically, your client who may have an axe to grind, may want to share the information with her ex-husband's employer or co-workers to embarrass him. This type of bad judgment is what gets Private Investigators in problem situations. Make sure your reports state that the information is sensitive and was prepared for your client only and should not be shared or disseminated with any third party.

As Investigators and owners of agencies, we get requests for video content and reports, sometimes from people or companies who were not our clients to begin with but who are involved in the same litigation and may also be defendants. Before, providing them with any information you must call your client and if you have a release, have them sign the release clearing you to share the evidence they paid you to develop. Keep in mind that this release does not bar you from charging a retrieval fee, copying or administration charges.

In other unrelated matters, you should not release any information until you are served a subpoena or received a signed release from the person who is or was the subject of the inquiry.

If a client requests a copy of the investigative report, video and evidence this should be done as a matter of practice and procedure, usually within a week's time of the conclusion of your investigation. Every client should receive a written report and invoice for service. They should never have to ask when they will be getting the report because you are behind in your work.

If evidence is being release from the office to be used at a hearing or trial then the investigator involved in the matter should submit a chain of custody form to the custodian of records.

Chain of Custody Procedure/ Evidence Tampering

Documenting the source of the evidence and keeping it safe is a high priority. Surveillance video is not edited or it may create the appearance that the evidence was tampered with to unfairly misrepresent the subject. Lets say you shoot video of a subject working and every time he stops to rub his back or take a break, you stop the video and back up to record just activity of his working and it appears he never took a break or was bothered by his injury.

Learning how to secure and not contaminate evidence is very important and will pertain to the type of cases you work. Items that are biodegradable should be stored in paper bags sealed and marked appropriately. Other items may be stored in sealed plastic bags. How you pick up and handle items is also important and gets a bit more complicated than this course is prepared to go into. Evidence collection is an entire area of study and many police department have crime scene investigators and evidence collectors.

Knowing your industry and how to prepare and control the evidence is crucial. In claims investigations, the evidence is submitted by the investigators immediately following the investigation and is marked with the subject name, file number date of collection and length of video. The video is then logged into the evidence locker of the agency and secured from any tampering. This record of transfer from the investigator to the office is called the chain of evidence or chain of custody. A letter of the chain of evidence may need to be produced when the case goes to trial and the video is produced as evidence.

Below is a real sample of a letter prepared by Claims Resource for an actual trial.

December 1, 2008

Video Evidence Chain of Custody letter

REF   Subject : Edward Murphy File

The following original video tapes have been removed from the evidence locker and hand delivered to Michael Martof for the hearing on December 2, 2008

As the evidence custodian the following six tapes are in their natural unedited state handed in by the investigators after each surveillance date and logged into our evidence locker. As the custodian of this evidence none of the tapes have been altered in any manner.

Videotape Log #	Investigator	Format
03-335	Clint Shonrock	8mm
03-409	Wendy Crane	8mm
03-452	Wendy Crane	8mm
05-172	Chuck Tiedman	miniDV

(The above four tapes have been copied on CD #1)

CD #2 contains Mr. Martof's videotape for both days. The CD copy is an exact duplicate of the originals.

07-183	Michael Martof	miniDV
07-190	Michael Martof	miniDV

The videotape evidence submitted above, original (format) & prepared CD have not been edited or manipulated in any manner.

Sincerely

John Bilyk
Custodian of Evidence

Chapter Five
The Private Investigator

- I. Who are Private Investigators
- II. What Private Investigators Do?
- III. What Makes a Good Private Investigator
    - a. Personal Qualifications of Successful Investigators/Surveillants
        - i. Ability to Function Unnoticed
        - ii. Physical Stamina
        - iii. Good Eyesight and Hearing
        - iv. Patience and Perseverance
        - v. Acting out a Role
        - vi. Good Judgment
        - vii. Self Confidence and Self Reliance
        - viii. Ability to Remember
- IV. What Type of Training is Available
- V. What Types of Advanced Training and Professional Certifications are there within the Industry?
- VI. How Does a Private Investigator Dress for Work
- VII. How Does a PI Break into the Industry

5. Who are Private Investigators?

According to the U.S. Department of Labor Bureau of Labor Statistics Private detectives and investigators assist individuals, businesses, and attorneys by finding and analyzing information. They connect small clues to solve mysteries or to uncover facts about legal, financial, or personal matters. Private detectives and investigators offer many services, including executive, corporate, and celebrity protection; pre-employment verification; and individual background profiles. Some investigate computer crimes, such as identity theft, harassing e-mails, and illegal downloading of copyrighted material. They also provide assistance in criminal and civil liability cases, insurance claims and fraud, child custody and protection cases, missing person's cases, and premarital screening. They are sometimes hired to investigate individuals to prove or disprove infidelity.

What Private Investigators Do

Private detectives and investigators have many methods to choose from when determining the facts in a case. Much of their work is done using a computer, recovering deleted e-mails and documents, for example. They may also perform computer database searches or work with someone who does. Computers allow investigators to quickly obtain huge amounts of information such as a subject's prior arrests, convictions, and civil legal judgments; telephone numbers; motor vehicle registrations; property ownership; association and club memberships; and even photographs.

Detectives and investigators also perform various other types of surveillance or searches. To verify facts, such as an individual's income or place of employment, they may make phone calls or visit a subject's workplace. In other cases, especially those involving missing persons and background checks, investigators interview people to gather as much information as possible about an individual. Sometimes investigators go undercover, pretending to be someone else to get information or to observe a subject inconspicuously.

Most detectives and investigators are trained to perform physical surveillance, which may be high-tech or low-tech. They may observe a site, such as the home of a subject, from an inconspicuous location or a vehicle. Using photographic and video cameras, binoculars, and cell phones, detectives often use surveillance to gather information on an individual; this can be quite time consuming.

The duties of private detectives and investigators depend on the needs of their clients. In cases that involve fraudulent workers' compensation claims, for example, investigators may carry out long-term covert observation of a person suspected of fraud. If an investigator observes him or her performing an activity that contradicts injuries stated in a worker's compensation claim, the investigator would take video to document the activity and report it to the client.

Detectives and investigators must be mindful of the law when conducting investigations. They keep up with Federal, State, and local legislation, such as privacy laws and other legal issues affecting their work. The legality of certain methods may be unclear, and investigators and detectives must make judgment calls when deciding how to pursue a case. They must also know how to collect evidence properly so that they do not compromise its admissibility in court.

Private detectives and investigators often specialize. Those who focus on intellectual property theft, for example, investigate and document acts of piracy, help clients stop illegal activity, and provide intelligence for prosecution and civil action. Other investigators specialize in developing financial profiles and asset searches. Their reports reflect information gathered through interviews, investigation, surveillance and research including review of public documents.

Computer forensic investigators specialize in recovering, analyzing, and presenting data from computers for use in investigations or as evidence. They determine the details of intrusions into computer systems, recover data from encrypted or erased files, and recover e-mails and deleted passwords.

Legal investigators assist in preparing criminal defenses, locating witnesses, serving legal documents, interviewing police and prospective witnesses, and gathering and reviewing evidence. Legal investigators also may collect information on the parties to the litigation, take photographs, testify in court, and assemble evidence and reports for trials. They often work for law firms or lawyers.

Corporate investigators conduct internal and external investigations for corporations. In internal investigations, they may investigate drug use in the workplace, ensure that expense accounts are not abused, or determine whether employees are stealing merchandise or information. External investigations attempt to thwart criminal schemes from outside the corporation, such as fraudulent billing by a supplier.

Financial investigators may be hired to develop confidential financial profiles of individuals or companies that are prospective parties to large financial transactions. These investigators often are certified public accountants (CPAs) who work closely with investment bankers and other accountants. They might also search for assets in order to recover damages awarded by a court in fraud or theft cases.

Detectives who work for retail stores or hotels are responsible for controlling losses and protecting assets. Store detectives, also known as loss prevention agents, safeguard the assets of retail stores by apprehending anyone attempting to steal merchandise or destroy store property. They prevent theft by shoplifters, vendor representatives, delivery personnel and even store employees. Store detectives also conduct periodic inspections of stock areas, dressing rooms, and restrooms, and sometimes assist in opening and closing the store. They may prepare loss prevention and security reports for management and testify in court against people they apprehend. Hotel detectives protect guests of the establishment from theft of their belongings and preserve order in hotel restaurants and bars. They also may keep undesirable individuals, such as known thieves, off the premises. (Most of the above examples DO NOT require licensure).

Work environment. Many detectives and investigators spend time away from their offices conducting interviews or doing surveillance, but some work in their office most of the day conducting computer searches and making phone calls. When the investigator is working on a case, the environment might range from plush boardrooms to seedy bars. Store and hotel detectives work in the businesses that they protect.

Investigators generally work alone, but they sometimes work with others during surveillance or when following a subject in order to avoid detection by the subject. Some of the work involves confrontation, so the job can be stressful and dangerous. Some situations call for the investigator to be armed, such as certain bodyguard assignments for corporate or celebrity clients. In most cases, however, a weapon is not necessary because the purpose of the work is gathering information and not law enforcement or criminal apprehension. Owners of investigative agencies have the added stress of having to deal with demanding and sometimes distraught clients.

Private detectives and investigators often work irregular hours because of the need to conduct surveillance and contact people who are not available during normal working hours. Early morning, evening, weekend, and holiday work is common.

Personal Qualifications of Successful Investigators/ Surveillants

The qualifications of good investigators/surveillants cover three areas: Physical, mental and resourcefulness, all of which enable the investigator to adapt to different situations.

Ability to Function Unnoticed

There should be nothing outstanding about the surveillant's appearance that would tend to attract attention. Blending with the environment in which the surveillance is to be conducted is one of the initial objectives of the investigator. The ability to blend in with and feel at home in a variety of environments and situations requires a high degree of adaptability and conformity.

Physical Stamina

Endurance is often a major factor in surveillance. Investigators may need to follow a person who is in excellent physical shape and moves rapidly without seeming to tire. In addition, surveillance operations are frequently prolonged, and they often involve tedious periods of waiting. Nonetheless, the investigator must remain on the alert; ready to act quickly when something finally does happen. The ability to put in long hours, to move quickly when necessary, and to do any one of a number of things over a long period to keep from losing track of a subject, all require stamina.

Good Eyesight and Hearing

Visual observation is the heart of surveillance, and therefore, good eyesight is essential. When viewing at great distances, binoculars, telescopes, and night viewing devices can assist the investigator. But always they must have keen eyes so they can quickly perceive and observant minds that can intelligently record what the eyes see. Investigators must register unanticipated movements of the subject so that they can take necessary counteraction.

Surveillance puts investigators' powers of observations to test. What the camera cannot record, the eyes of the investigator should register.

Keen hearing is also a definite plus factor. Occasionally, investigators may be close enough to overhear an informative bit of conversation, in a bar, restaurant, store or office, or on the street. When sitting on surveillance, the investigator should be listening for significant sounds such as sounds emitted from the subject's residence which would indicate that he may be inside working or working somewhere on the premises.

Driving Skills

The driver's eyesight, coordination and reflexes are all important. They determine the difference between immediate and delayed action. Surveillants' vehicles, like the surveillants, should blend into the general flow of traffic with nothing about them to cause them to stand out from other vehicle. Mental alertness and good judgment are the keys to driving adaptively in vehicular surveillance operations.

Resourcefulness

Resourcefulness is one of the most important qualifications for investigators. An investigator who is resourceful can quickly adapt to and successfully cope with changing conditions, unforeseen circumstances and direct challenges.

Patience and Perseverance

In this business, patience is a virtue. There are often tedious waiting periods before anything happens. Investigators must persevere—if one day's effort fails to bring the desired results, they must go at it again and again spite of outside influences and opposition.

Acting out a Role

In some type of surveillance, particularly in undercover work, the investigators have to become actors and take on the role of a corporation employee, secret organization member, salesperson, or other role they must assume to conduct a specific surveillance. They may pose as a telephone serviceman, brush salesman, cab drivers, corporate executives, drug addicts or simply fellow workers on the production lines. Whatever role is assumed carries with it the necessity of acting out that role so effectively that the surveillance activities go completely undetected.

In a disguised outdoor surveillance role, the surveillant investigators must appear to be what they purport to be in dress, manner, and performance. They should appear to be conducting business, delivery or repair service without revealing their interest in what others are doing. Investigators should be able to give a plausible, acceptable reason for being in a given place at a given time should their presence be challenged. With this type of setup, the investigator should have uniforms, I.D.'s, or other documents to support their claims.

Role-playing also includes the ability to talk one's way out of potentially embarrassing situations without creating suspicions should such explanations become necessary. The more effectively and inconspicuously the investigator is able to play the role, the less likely he is to arouse suspicion or be burned.

Knowledge and Good Judgment

All forms of investigation call for good judgment based on knowledge and common sense. Surveillance often puts good judgment and common sense to a real test. Such judgment is based on the background knowledge obtained in pre-surveillance preparation, on personal knowledge of surveillance techniques, and on the logical decisions to be made in different circumstances. Only knowledge can determine the most appropriate technique. Good judgment can tell when and how to apply it.

Self Confidence and Self Reliance

Self confidence and self reliance are good psychological attitudes and traits for investigators to have, enabling them to take on assignments with confidence and rely on their own abilities to cope with any situations that might arise. The more competent one becomes, the more confident one is.

Ability to Remember

Investigators need a good memory. This is especially true on a foot surveillance or when conducting an activities check. Undercover investigators never record information while in the presence of a fellow employee or associate whom they have been assigned to observe. During mobile surveillance and during the observation of a subject who is extremely active, it is not always possible to record information simultaneously. The longer the interval between gathering and recording the information the greater the recall problem. While observations and evidential information should always be recorded at the earliest convenience, some situations are such that this cannot be done until a later time. It is then that the memory and recall ability are very important. Memory can be continually improved by constant exercise and practice.

What Type of Training is Available

Most companies will train you the way they want you to do things. You need to know the basics which will mean practicing, and reading up on whatever type of specialty you decide on pursuing. If your specialty compliments a former vocation then you will just need to learn the formalities of transitioning your talents to offer then in the private sector for a fee. If you have no talent other than pure ambition then you will most likely be a quick learner and study ever aspect of this and any other how to manual you can get your hands on. The simple truth is that private investigation work is a lot of common sense and problem solving put together one piece at a time. Common sense is not something you learn and many investigators will tell you they never stop learning as each case is different. The benefit new investigators have to day is the internet. Just about everything you may need to know about a particular type of case may be at your finger tips in a Google search. For example if you are investigator to try and find out of a guy is an over the road trucker, you can Google, what does it take to be an over the road trucker. What licenses do I need to have and what certifications do I need. These searches and the answers will start your investigation off in one direction or another and upon being thorough, you will most likely get all of the information you need to prove your case. At one time, I needed to refer to a how to guide and if that type of case was not in there I was on my own. With the internet you are never really on your own.

Advanced Training and Professional Certifications

Continuing Education is always recommended and should be sought out through a local statewide or national association for reputable training and certification. FALI, the Florida Association of Legal Investigators is a great place to start. Some of other national designations available are CFE, Certified Fraud Examiner and Certified Legal Investigator CLI. These National Certifications and Examination are usually recommended for investigators with at least three years of experience. There is also the Board Certified Criminal Defense Investigator, Insurance Fraud Investigator, Legal Investigator, Fire Investigator and Certified Surveillance Investigator.

The PI School offers the Certified Surveillance Investigator certification through a separate advanced field work program.

While Florida does not **yet** have mandatory CEU's the local association conferences offer great resources for continuing education and information about updated products and services to assist the professional investigator.

There is also a large Insurance and Department of Insurance Fraud (DIF) Conference annually in Orlando with professional speakers, instructors and investigators offering continuing education as part of the three day conference. There will also be many professional investigations agencies setting up marketing booths and offering their services to the insurance industry.

Dress for Work

If you are out doing SIU or statement work and meeting people, then business casual is required. If you are taking statements from other professionals, then you should dress up to their level. I once had a doctor who I wanted to take a statement from and he was offended that I was not wearing a suit coat and tie. So understand that you attire is important and may stand in the way of getting your job done. During the initial appointment setting ask them if it is okay that you will be dressed in a company polo shirt and slacks or whether they require a suit and tie.

On surveillance the dress the dress is comfortably casual and you should even bring a backup set of clothing. You may sweat through the first set but the second reason for bringing a change of clothes is so you have them incase the subject heads out of town while you're following him. Never leave your subject when he is on the move. In thirty years, I have never been stiffed with the costs of travel or extra time when I followed a person out of town In fact to the contrary, I have been given cart blanche. I once followed a claimant from Tampa to Nevada and onto California, where the claimant took his family to Disney land over Easter. Needless to say, I hadn't packed for the occasion, but I had been in this situation before and it's always nice to know you can get a complete change of clothes at Wal-Mart for about $15.00.

Anyway, clothes are important as are the shoes you are wearing. Many companies prohibit the wearing of flip flops which have been very popular of late. Unfortunately they just don't protect your feet if you need to go into the woods or move quickly to run after someone. To have a pair in your bag is fine but if you work near the beach, but the preferred shoe is a rubber soled shoe or sneakers.

The investigator's clothing line does not stop here though. There should be a camouflaged bag in the truck that contains more essentials of the investigator on the move. This bag should be filled with camouflage clothing. A camouflage hat, possible mosquito hat and even a large camouflage netting.

You should also have bug spray in the bag, toilet paper, pepper spray, and a pair of pruning clippers in case you need to build a blind where one is sparse or doesn't exist. And finally the most important item, a seat. Many hunting supply stores and even Wal-Mart sells a three legged stool or folding chair with a small collapsible cooler underneath in the sporting good s/hunting section of the store. For the clothes and back pack and netting get these from your local Army Navy Store. Also don't forget to bring your monopod and tripod and if you know before hand you are going into the woods, stop for drinks, food and some snacks.

Our goal in surveillance is to get in the best position possible to watch our subject. This may mean a position in the hot son. There are those investigators who constantly look for shade trees to sit under and seem to be more conscientious of their comfort rather than the results of their efforts. If results are your number one priority and they should be, then you will in fact find yourself sitting in the sun. We need to learn to stay cool. Avoid using your air-conditioning in your car to and from cases. This will help acclimate your body to the outside temperature. Get a fan that runs of solar power can be put in your window. Use deodorant not antiperspirant, you want to sweat this is your body's natural cooling system. An antiperspirant blocks your under arm sweat glands prohibiting them from releasing sweat to cool the body, not the most ideal situation .

How do You Break into The Industry

As previously stated the need for PI's is continuing to increase. Many will parlay prior experience and offer an array of services. Some will join existing companies Another way to start is to find an existing firm and invest in it or take it over from a retiring owner. In any instance, you will need to have a business plan for getting cases.

Businesses of every type have trade shows and educational conferences. These are the areas where the prospective PI business will sponsor portions of the event or set up a booth to market their services. Sponsorships can vary from $250.00 – $5, 000 and up. Booth costs at a trade show can start at around $800.00 and cost upwards of $3000.00. For the Insurance industry there are a number of conferences and trade shows. For instance the Workers Compensation Claims Profession WCCP has a web site with posted events and can be found at www.wwccp.org. They have an Annual Claims Manager Conference in June just to name one but also have a huge show in August every year. The SIU professional also links up with the Florida Division of Insurance Fraud each year in June for an annual DIF/SIU joint conference. Booths and sponsorships at all levels can be purchased to advertise and market your business.

I have an old friend that has been in business for about 25 years. His wife was a very successful programmer and she moved from time to time as like she liked to say, "she was the bread winner of the family". Gil as we liked to call him though knew differently. He knew the money he was spending on soccer lessons for his sons would pay for college and while he was a part-time stay at home Dad, he was also a career PI. But it's tough to substantiate yourself when you move often. Well I asked Gil how he gets business for himself, then the stories started. He did subcontractor work or worked part-time for other agencies sometimes those with out of state offices looking for an experienced person in his area by calling local PI firms and those out of the state. And when he was going to be in an area for a year or longer, he applied for his own state PI agency License. Now this also happened several times and Gil advised that he would go to companies and "hang out" in the smoking areas and meet adjusters as they took a smoke break. Gil would state he a was a PI and on a marketing call to drum up business. He was very personable, funny and entertaining. He would follow-up with his visit and also the people he met in the smoking area until he wedged himself in there for some work. In my experience, you need to have a niche market or specialty.

Chapter Six
Locate Investigations

6. Locate Investigations Guideline

Many investigations will require the knowledge of how to locate someone. As soon as I am asked to conduct a locate investigation, I immediately review all the information the client provided. Many times the key to finding the subject will be in the information provided. The client may say they checked the subject former address and they are no loner there. But this address may have been a rental and the client never thought to identify the landlord or owner of the property and call them for a forwarding address.

Do not hesitate to ask your client for additional information after you have reviewed the information they provided. Keep them involved with the investigation and where it's going. You do not want to report something to your client, after several days of hard work, only to discover that a particular fact was already known by your client. Unfortunately, your client won't tell you everything in the first interview. Not that they're trying to hide things from you but, what you may consider important clues in your investigation, they will not. That's why you must make them part of what you're doing and keep them up to date. Also, if they are part of the decision-making process and a given decision costs then more time and money, it is easier for them to accept the extra charges.

Always remember that most anyone can be found. The professional investigator is only limited by time and money- never their imagination. The steps listed in this lesson are part of the methodology of investigation for a locate investigation on a subject whose moved. It is not intended to cover the steps for an abducted person or child.

Pay special attention to this step—by—step locate investigation and you will find that these are very similar to the steps utilized when conducting a thorough background investigation in relation to your subject. Always keep in mind that investigative work is both scientific and artistic in its application. Learn how to use the resources available to you effectively.

Americans move from place to place more than any other nation of people. Twenty-five percent of us move every year. We move to take advantage of new employment or a business opportunity, to change our lifestyle, to continue our education, or to be closer to our families and friends. To think that every locate assignment you get will be like finding a needle in a haystack would be highly incorrect. Most of the times, we are hired because our clients just don't have the time or know where to begin to look.

Although I know I may be forgetting a case or two, it's actually really difficult for me to recall not being able to locate a person my client sought. I would imagine most of my competitors would say the same thing because that's just the nature of our business. Your only limitations are usually time, money and imagination. The fact is, given unlimited resources; a person's face could be plastered all over the TV one evening and within hours of the first broadcast you may find the phone ringing off the hook with where that missing person was two minutes earlier with precise accuracy. After all, remember, most people we attempt to locate as investigators are lost friends, relatives, former employee who witnesses an accident, or our client's client. These subjects are not on the list of America's Most Wanted. Also, there is a high probability that the investigator will be able to locate a good address for the subject just by running their name in one of our national databases.

Again you need to keep in mind that we are typically looking for ordinary citizens. They are not missing person cases, thank GOD. Just in Florida there are an estimated 9,000 Private Investigators and this would be a very sad world if we worked child abductions cases every day. Don't get me wrong, nationally, missing and exploited children is a growing problem. However organizations like The National Center for Missing & Exploited Children have worked hard with Law Enforcement to dramatically increase the recovery rate for missing children to roughly 90% today. Organizations like this have specific procedures in place and work with the missing child's family and local law enforcement.
As a "For-Hire" Investigator most of your casework will come from business clients such as Attorney Firms, Corporations and Insurance Companies looking for witnesses, defendants and former employees.

The following are step—by—step procedures the professional investigator uses in a standard locate investigation.

STEP 1: The first step of your locate investigation is to simply run a database search with a reputable database firm offered by companies like Lexis Nexis, or TLO. Although we are looking for the most current address on file, don't overlook the oldest address identified either. If the newest address is one that has already been determined to be invalid or no longer good, move your attention to some of the oldest addresses. Many times you will find the oldest address is that of a parent or grandparent. In all cases you are looking for telephone numbers verified and unverified that can be called to inquire about the whereabouts of the subject. Remember we want to first do as much work as we can without leaving our office.

STEP 2: Utilizing your same database run just the address and leave the search name blank. This will identify all of the people who lived at that address over time. What you are looking for is the name of a subject appearing during the same time period your subject was also reported to be at the same address. This overlapping information may indicate that our subject resided at that location with a roommate, family member, ex-spouse or friend. Also, always look for any telephone numbers listed for any subject associated to our subjects address and call every number.

STEP 3: Your next step is to cross reference your subject as well as anyone else identified as a possible associate through the sunbiz.org corporate and business database. This will identify any potential businesses your subject or a related person may be involved in. Remember we are not just looking for Corporations, but also fictitious name filings as well. The broadest search tool should be used in each category by searching under Officers and Registered Agents. Once again any business entity should be contacted. Look through the corporate filings or annual reports for telephone numbers listed on the bottom of the pages as contact numbers for the business. Search the Internet for any website under that business name and query the Contact Us Page to send email requests. Google each person's name to identify any other pertinent information that may be available on-line and follow any lead identified. On-line county tax roll records will help you to determine whether your subject owns any real, personal or business property in that county. The Property Appraiser's Office will identify the property address, value and recorded deed and mortgage. Your next search on-line will include criminal records. County Court Criminal records should be available on-line. Here, you are going to check your subject's name for any convictions under both misdemeanor and felony divisions. If your subject has a record, his or her file folder will contain additional information. The full file can be reviewed in-person by making a personal visit to the courthouse. Criminal records can contain vital information such as known aliases, employers and telephone numbers. Court documents will also provide specific information regarding the charges brought against your subject. Don't forget to check the traffic court. Oftentimes, the traffic court is located in the misdemeanor division of the courthouse. If your subject has received a traffic ticket and you can obtain a copy of it, the traffic ticket will tell you what your subject was driving and list your subject's address at that time. They may even have a scanned copy of the envelope he mailed in his payment with containing a return address. Next, the civil division will be of help to you. Here, you are going to check for any suits filed against your subject, or any suits your subject may have filed. The civil division will also record any liens against your subject, the subject's property or any liens that your subject may have filed against others. The civil division also contains records of marriage and divorce. Occupational licenses can also be searched in person or on-line if available to identify any business the subject may have in the county or city. Also, check the Uniform Commercial Code (UCC) filings in the civil division. A UCC filing is for loans secured with collateral, such as machinery, equipment and any asset that may not have a title or registration. Once again, discovering this paperwork may lead you to a better address for the subject you are looking for or possibly even an unknown business he operates based on the type of collateralized equipment he has loans for. Also, check with the probate court in the city where the subject was last known to reside. The probate court will be a source for any wills your subject may have filed or be the executor of and any adoptions or guardianships your subject may be involved in.

STEP 4: By this point we have already located about 90 percent of the people we have been requested to locate. However if we still haven't found your subject we will need to step it up a notch and invoke some help. Without a doubt the social website of Facebook has dramatically changed the landscape of social interaction.

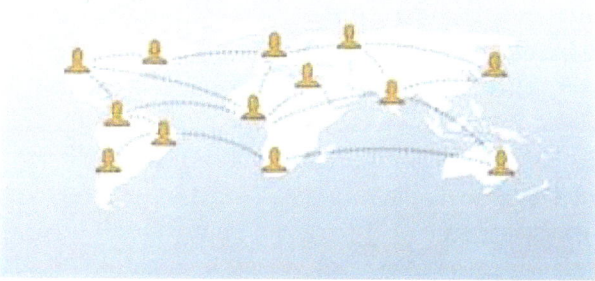

We can now not only look for the subject on Facebook, but we can solicit all of his or her friends to have the source contact us. Power in numbers is a great thing and don't be shy about the numbers part! Ask as many of his/her "friends" to tell the source we need to speak to them and to call us or even ask if someone has a contact number or email. I was recently hired to find several former employees of a company who witnessed a slip and fall accident. The employee's personnel files had been reviewed and there were no clues to determine their locations. I found two of the four rather quickly, secured their statements and then moved on to the other two searching them on Facebook. One of the subject's was identified as living in Atlanta but the other subject seemed to have a more checkered address history and still alluded me. He had been evicted from his last two addresses and the landlords of each had no idea of his current whereabouts or were reluctant to get involved. In one of the evictions I found it was an out of state uncle who actual owned the condominium and evicted his nephew. I elicited the help of about ten of his "friends" on Facebook. Prior to this I had already found his mother, uncle and grandfather. I spoke to all of the sources and while I felt they knew where he lived, they were unwilling to assist me. When I did not get an immediate reply from anyone on Facebook, I put the names of each family member and their addresses in my report and suggested that subpoenas be directed to their attention as they had indicated to me several times that they were in occasional contact with the subject I needed to locate. I considered this a completed assignment 3.5 out of 4 until four months went by and out of the blue, the subject calls me as says, "I heard you are looking for me". The real truth was that I had long closed that file, but wanting to improve my record to 100 percent, I took down his current address and telephone number and sent it to my client!

STEP 5: In more difficult cases a post office box may be the only address you find. In these cases, I usually go to the counter and advise I am attempting to serve the subject or locate them for pending litigation. I simply show my private investigators ID and let them do the rest of the assuming. In these cases, the less you say the better. In order to maintain a Post Office Box, a physical address MUST be on file. If the Postmaster shows me the address and I already know it is no longer valid I tell them so. I ask the Postmaster if he will lock the mailbox so that when the subject comes to the Post Office he won't be able to access his mail box and is forced to come to the counter to inquire about his mail. Sometimes they just hold the mail and place a card inside the box saying "see Post Office Supervisor". Either way the subject is forced to the counter at which point the Postmaster can advise the subject that they need an updated address. Prior to leaving, I ask the Postmaster if I can call him in a week's time to get the subject's update physical address. While this delays your case for a while, it usually works like clockwork and saves you from needing to stake out the Post Office Box waiting for the subject to come check their mail.

I have also found not to ever overlook the value of the local postal carrier who services the route of your subject's last known address. If they are in the area during your visit of the last known address, make sure you speak to them. They see your subject's mail and if you don't think they pay attention you're wrong. They know a lot about the people they deliver to; some know more than others, but always talk to them. They often know what type of car your subject drives, and possibly where they work. When questioning the postal carrier be polite, sincere and don't forget to say thank you.

STEP 6: If I still haven't found the subject, then I need to get even more aggressive. I need to refocus on what I know about where he used to work and live. The subject's past employer or employees the subject worked with are all valuable sources of information and may still be in touch with the subject. The subject's previous landlord or apartment manager may provide valuable information as to where they are. They may have a copy of a lease application filled out by the subject containing information such as references or a nearest relative's contact information. Any known friends or associates of the subject may have the key to where the subject is hiding. If the subject has an ex-husband or wife, and you can locate them, they may be very willing to give you a current address or provide information that will assist you.

STEP 7: Make a personal visit to the physical neighborhood of the subject's last known address. The subject may not have left a forwarding address at the post office for his mail but, most likely, he made friends with some people in the area before moving out. These neighbors may have maintained contact with the subject and know where he or she is living at this time. When conducting this type of face—to—face canvas; don't forget the children that you see in the area. Children have a habit of being very honest and forthcoming with information when questioned in the right way. Now, when I say question the children in the neighborhood, keep in mind that you must exercise extreme discretion when attempting to do this. Don't drive down the streets of suburban America in your black sedan, roll down the window and ask children to come over to your car. Use your head and let common sense prevail.

I was once assigned to locate a subject and after reviewing the subject's file, I initiated a neighborhood canvas at the subject's last known address. The residents at this address turned out to be the subject's family members, his mother, father, brothers and sisters. As I approached the residence, there were several young children, approximately nine or ten years old, playing baseball in the front yard. I walked up to the front yard, picked up the baseball and started playing catch with the kids. After five or ten minutes and a couple of pitches later, I asked one of the children if Johnny, my subject, was home. The child stated to me that his brother Johnny hadn't lived at home for over a year. The child then continued to tell me that his brother, Johnny, had moved out to Colorado and was a cook at a ski lodge called the Big Bear. Moments later, I proceeded to the residence and knocked on the door. The door was answered by Johnny's mother. Using an appropriate pretext, I asked the subject's mother if Johnny was home or if she knew where I could reach him. She stated to me that she hadn't seen her son for well over a year and that he was nothing but trouble. For the next five minutes, she continued to tell me what a disappointment her son had been, repeating she had no contact with him and had no idea where he was. Keep in mind that when you question sources close to your subject, such as relatives or friends, they may try to cover up the truth. As I got back to my office, I looked up the Big Bear and found a Colorado Resort by that name on the Internet. I obtained a telephone number for the resort, called up and asked for the restaurant. I spoke with a hostess at the restaurant and asked for Johnny. The hostess told me that she didn't think he was in yet but to hold on and she would check the schedule. She returned moments later and informed me that Johnny was scheduled to begin work that afternoon at 4:00 p.m. She told me that Johnny was a cook and worked Tuesday through Sunday from 4:00 p.m. until closing.

Following a specific plan of action, I made a personal visit to Johnny's last known address to conduct a thorough canvass of the area. I found this residence to be Johnny's parent's house. Here I discreetly question Johnny's little brother who gave me the information I felt was valid. Had I not gotten the information from Johnny's brother, I would have been much more aggressive with his parents. Parents, despite their differences, usually know how to reach their children.

STEP 8: You may have a list of cases, you need to further investigate and the actual files can only be reviewed by making a personal visit to the county courthouse. Each county courthouse is different and while most are on-line, the record you see online will only be a brief fraction of the information you can get by pulling and reviewing the actual paper file. If you are in a small county be extremely polite and courteous you will get more assistance with a pleasant attitude. You should also be thinking about developing a friend on the inside you can call to obtain information instead of making the drive. The best investigators are always developing their sources.

STEP 9: Hopefully, by following this step—by—step location guide, you have found your subject by now. Remember that the subject's social security can establish which state your subject applied for his or her social security account. It is usually your subject's home state, a state your subject may return to, especially in times of trouble. Your subject may have friends or relatives to stay with or be near or from which to receive assistance. Somewhere during your investigation, a city or town in that state may have been uncovered or mentioned in passing that will help lead you to your subject.

STEP 10: A motor vehicle registration or MVR record search can usually be obtained on the subject at the County Tax Office. These records are also part of the typical database search run through Nexis Lexis or TLO. This information is generally available to the public, although it is considered protected information by a handful of states. Any license plate numbers associated to your subject should be ran to identify the owner. You may have a tag of a car your subject was seen driving in or obtained a ticket in for speeding. The Tag can be cross—referenced to identify the owner's name, date of birth and address.

STEP 11: State driver's license, or DL information, is also commonly accessed by the professional investigator. Driver's license information can be obtained in virtually every state, with a few exceptions. Certain states restrict access by requiring that you have your subject's driver's license number before they will give you any information. This number can be obtained from the database report ran in STEP 1. With the driver's license information, you can determine whether or not your subject has a valid license. It may also show tickets from another state indicating he has moved. Many county courthouses throughout the state sell 7 & 12 year DL records. Call ahead and make certain you are not wasting a trip to the courthouse. These records are also available online through your database source or another on-line specialty search company for a fee.

STEP 12: The local or city utility department is also a good source for locating your subject. Many times these utility services are county run businesses and as such their records are available for review. If the information from the local utility department is not readily accessible to the general public then consider developing an inside source whenever possible.

STEP 13: If you've followed all these steps and are still unable to locate your subject, don't overlook the Department of Corrections, the DOC. Your subject may be receiving three square meals a day, safe and sound in a state correctional facility. With your subject's name and social security number, you can query the supervised population database of the Department of Corrections (DOC) in virtually every state across the country and determine whether your subject is incarcerated at this time. The same holds true for the federal prison system.

STEP 14: If you still have not found the subject of your investigation, call the Bureau of Vital Statistics or double check your database to see if you see DOD after his name indicating the Date of Death. This information is obtained from the SSN Death Benefits database usually part of most national comprehensive databases.

Chapter Seven
Surveillance

I. Surveillance
   A. Covert and Overt Surveillance
   B. Types of Surveillance
      1. Fixed or Stationary Surveillance
      2. Mobile or Moving Surveillance
         a. Loose Tail
         b. Close Tail
   C. Pre-surveillance Preparation
      1. Positive Identification
         a. Photograph
         b. Description
         c. Observation
      2. Personal Data
      3. Subject's Lifestyle
      4. Purpose of Investigation
      5. Surveillance Territory
      6. Plan the Surveillance
      7. Equipment

II. Observation Posts and Stationary Surveillance
   A. Selecting Observations Posts
      1. Surveillance Movements
      2. Equipment
      3. Inside Surveillance
      4. Outside Surveillance Post
      5. Surveillance Rural Area

III. Automobile Surveillance
   A. Selecting Surveillance Vehicles
      1. Avoid Vehicles that Attract Attention
      2. Good Operating Condition
   B. Conducting Surveillance
      1. Initiating Surveillance
      2. Surveillance Do's
      3. Surveillance Don'ts

IV. Daily Surveillance Check List
   A. Preliminary Surveillance Investigation
   B. Arrival, Subject's Residence
   C. Canvass Neighborhood
   D. Take up Surveillance Position
   E. Observations

7. SURVEILLANCE

Mobile surveillance is the covert (concealed), and constant watch of a subject while following the subject on foot or in a vehicle. Stationary surveillance is the observation of a subject or location from a fixed vantage point. Many times this position is concealed in the woods where camouflage clothing is worn or a natural "blind" is made from the surrounding tree branches and debris to blend in with your surroundings. The goal of course is to remain undetected in your position to afford the greatest opportunity to observe your subject in their natural state.

The key to any successful surveillance is to enter and exit the area without anyone knowing you where there.

The investigator who functions, as a covert observer is known as a surveillant. The "subject" is the person, under observation. <u>The art of surveillance is the investigator's ability to conduct observation of this nature without the subject ever being made aware of the surveillance.</u>

Surveillance is a form of direct observation. The investigators personally and directly observe the activities of the subject and any information thereby disclosed.

1. <u>Stationary/fixed Surveillance</u>

In fixed surveillance the investigators (surveillants) observe from a fixed observation post. Fixed surveillance is used in the surveillance of places and of persons who frequent those places. In our business, fixed surveillances are usually conducted from a parked vehicle or from a surveillance position on foot, which affords a better view of the residence where our subject resides.

A fixed or stationary surveillance can very suddenly become a moving surveillance if the subject decides to leave the area, either on foot or by vehicle. However in many instances, an investigator may need to decide whether the surveillance will remain stationary or whether mobile surveillance will even be an option. In some instances it is not practical to attempt to do both. This is sometimes the case in very rural areas where the only discreet position will be a stationary one in the woods. In these cases it is advised to park your vehicle at a busy location where other vehicles are parked or be dropped off in the woods by a second investigator. A car parked in a remote area too close to your surveillance position will surely tip off any savvy subject.

2. Mobile or Moving Surveillance

Mobile surveillance occurs when both the subject and the surveillants are on the move by foot, in a vehicle, or in public transportation. Obviously moving surveillance makes great demands on the resourcefulness of the surveillant.

In a moving surveillance the investigators follow the subject, either on foot or in a suitable vehicle and tracks their every move all while observing any significant events, contacts, or activities, or any bit of evidence that the subject may inadvertently disclose to the surveillant.

3. Degrees of Moving Surveillance

Various degrees of moving surveillance are indicated by such terms as loose tail, close tail, open tail, rough tail. The nature of the case, the type of information needed, and the importance of continuous surveillance are all factors that help to determine the degree of persistent observation maintained.

a. Loose Tail

A loose tail, or loose surveillance is a cautious procedure that is performed to obtain general information about the subject's activities, associates, and habits without running great risk of being detected. In other words, the subject is followed loosely; it is not as persistent as the close tail.

b. Close Tail

Close surveillance tends to pursue the operation at any cost, within reason. The subject is kept under close observation at all times, even when the risk of discovery is high. The importance of the information to be learned may warrant that risk.

In our business the degree of surveillance should fall somewhere in between the loose tail surveillance and the close tail surveillance.

B. PRESURVEILLANCE PREPARATION

Success or failure depends largely on the surveillant's ability and resourcefulness in preparation for, and performance of surveillance activities. Maximum preparation paves the way for maximum performance. The adequately prepared usually succeed; the unprepared are almost sure to fail.

Too many times surveillants have relied on old information or addresses provided by adjusters, attorneys and others who are not completely in the know. This results in wasteful valuable and embarrassing hours of hanging around watching a house from which the subject moved two or three weeks ago. A quick phone call to the individual's home the night before, a check with directory assistance or a spot check or some pre-surveillance work during the week before is well worthwhile in avoiding such a catastrophe. It is usually not necessary to visit the neighborhood before a surveillance or call, however, if other pre-surveillance investigation leads the surveillant to believe that the subject may not reside at the address, then further pre-surveillance investigation is necessary.

The more information one has about the person to be followed, the more likelihood there is of the investigator being able to adjust intelligently to the subject's activities and unexpected moves. Knowledge of the subject's habits, associates, appointments, favorite places to go, business and social ties and friends and relatives can help the investigator pick up the subject's trail after temporarily losing it.

Whenever a surveillant has been detected he has not only wasted his valuable time, he has alerted the subject to the fact that he has been placed under observation.

Surveillants should have a prior knowledge of the following if possible:

1. The subject, the specific person or place to be surveilled.

2. The area in which the surveillance is to be conducted.

3. The specific objective of the surveillance.

4. The circumstances under which the investigator will have to function.

5. The type of surveillance.

   1. Positive Identification

Certainty of the subject's identification is obviously the first rule of surveillance. Investigators must be sure that they positively know the identity of their subject so as not to waste time and effort following the wrong person.

There are three procedures for securing a subject's appearance identification. As far as it is possible to do so, investigators should have:

1. A recent photograph of the subject provided by the client or previous investigation done by another agency.

2. A complete description of the subject.

3. Close personal observation of the subject.

Recent photographs, when available, can be very helpful, particularly full-length photographs that allow examination of the posture, build, height and weight of the subject. It is unusual that our clients provide us with a photograph of the subject. However, if the case was worked by another investigator in the office, it is possible that video or still images or available to review. It is best to obtain a complete description of the subject from more than one person. Good descriptions are sometimes hard to come by; however, they are essential and when more than one is obtained comparison of the descriptions may prove helpful. Descriptions of a person one has never met are especially valuable when they include a significant personal characteristic or habit that distinguishes the subject from others.

Quite often the client does have a full description of the subject, however, if they do not the information is available through other sources. If there is an attorney representing the insured, he may have taken a deposition and had the opportunity to observe the subject. He then could describe the subject. If neither the client nor the attorney have a physical description, it is possible to obtain a physical description from the insured or a rehabilitation worker. However, before contacting either one authorization should be gotten from the client.

Please be aware that it is not always possible to get a physical description though the surveillance has to be initiated in spite of it.

A casual introduction to ID the subject is a more sensitive situation. The surveillant must never be obvious about it. If at all possible, it is best to have someone else point the subject out to the investigator so that the investigator does not have any personal confrontation with the subject. When it is necessary for the investigator to personally contact the subject, it should be done in a casual manner, very natural, and the investigator should make every effort to identify the subject without creating suspicion on the part of the subject.

An investigator should always try to avoid any personal confrontation with a subject during the early stages of the investigation.

Most observations will be made while looking at the subject from behind. Any physical characteristics identifiable from behind are excellent tailing identification factors. Surveillants can watch the subject from behind after they have identified his face in person. Check for characteristics of appearance and movements. Is there anything about the subject's posture or build or in the way he carries himself, gestures he makes, or the way he holds his head? What about his gait, the speed and manner of his walking? Other things to look for are as follows: Does the subject usually go bare headed? What is the color of his hair? How does it appear from the back? Or does the subject wear hats, or caps? If so, what type, style and color are they? Is the subject bald or partially bald? What, if any, portion of his baldness can be seen from behind? Is his hair long or short? If long, does it reach his shoulders? Or is it cut high up the neck?

If the subject is a woman, the style as well as the color of the hair should be noted. Investigators should compose a complete mental image of the subject as he appears from behind. Are his shoulders massive with his head set close to them? Or does he have narrow shoulders and a long neck? Is there anything unusual about the way in which he walks, stands or moves? Is his walk quick and firm, or slow and hesitant: Is his carriage erect and straight, or does he sway from side to side? Does he lean forward or is he stooped over: Is there anything unusual about the subject's appearance? What actions, gestures, or habits are noticeable? Analyze the subject's entire form and movements from behind and note carefully and clearly visible identifiable physical or moving characteristics that can be readily viewed and quickly detected from behind. Some subjects will have more pronounced identification clues than others.

2. Personal Data

In addition to knowing what the subject looks like, it is particularly important to know who the subject actually is. A second rule of preparation is to get all available personal data on the subject:

1. Full name, nicknames, and any aliases.

2. Residence, address and telephone number.

3. Where the employed: Company name, address and telephone number.

4. Means of transportation: Owns car, public transportation, rides with someone else, or walks.

3. Subject's Lifestyles

The third rule of preparation is to learn as much as possible about the subject's lifestyle. This covers a wide area of relevant factors such as:

1. The subject's family, associates and friends.

2. Places he frequents.

3. His most noticeable habits.

4. Characteristics of his neighborhood.
5. Is he a family man, a loner, or has a girlfriend.

6. His reputation in the community.

It is always advisable to have the names and addresses of the subject's relatives, key associates and friends. Then, when the subject stops at one of their homes, the investigator will know who he is going to see or at least in whose home the subject is in at that particular time. If the investigator has previously looked up or acquired the telephone numbers of the subject's friends, associates, and relative, and places he frequents most and they lose track of him during a surveillance in any of these areas, they can make a "pretext" telephone call and learn if the subject is there and perhaps pick up on the subject again.

If possible, the surveillants should know the cars owned and driven by the subject, their model, year and license number.

The greater one's knowledge of the subject, the more prepared they'll be in following the subject.

4. Purpose of Investigation

Surveillants should know why the subject needs to be placed under surveillance. An investigator receiving a surveillance assignment should be fully informed about its purpose. The investigator should also know what specific information the client wants the investigator to obtain. He should also be aware of the exact instructions received from the client such as any monetary limits placed upon the investigation or limited amount of hours to be placed on the investigation. Usually the client will request whether or not they want videotape, still photographs or both if they subject is involved in any noteworthy activity. If there are any questions in the investigator's mind as to the purpose or the objectives of the surveillance, then the client should be contacted before any investigation is initiated.

5. Surveillance Territory

Familiarity with the areas and with the environment in which the assignment is to be conducted is essential.

There are three major steps to take to become familiar with the areas and locations in which surveillance is to be conducted:

1. Study maps of the areas.

2. Make a preliminary survey of the areas.

3. Closely observe the neighborhood environment.

Maps should be studied to determine the layout of the streets: Alleys and dead-end streets; main travel ways; freeways, turnpikes and their on and off ramps; apparent natural get-away routes and public transportation routes. Being familiar with the area is essential in moving surveillance. Map study, a personal survey and environmental information all combine to create a functional familiarity with the territory that enables the investigators to make quick, intelligent moves as required.

Driving through the street, it helps to take special note of parking and vacant lots, and service stations, fast food outlets and markets at intersections that would permit a quick transition from a street of traveling to a cross street. Driveways connecting two streets also provide useful throughways. The value of such quick bypass from one street to another to keep from being detained at a light or by unusual heavy traffic is quite helpful.

While surveying the neighborhood, the investigator should attempt to identify a point or address in the area where he believes the subject will first appear, whether it be at the subject's front door, car, someone else's residence, place of business, parking place, etc. The investigator should also determine if there are any other addresses in the nearby area where the subject might visit during the surveillance. If so, the investigator should map out the route that the subject is most likely to take.

Before conducting an automobile surveillance, it is advisable to drive around the streets in the immediate area in which the observation is expected to begin. The investigator should select a key vantage point (never in the same block as the subject's place) from which the investigator can readily observe the subject's place and wait and watch for his appearance.

If the subject lives in an area that is sparsely traveled or in a patrolled residential area, the investigator should not make their survey so obvious as to call attention to themselves or their vehicle. Pre-surveillance survey should be done as normally as possible, attracting as little attention as possible.

When establishing stationary surveillance, the survey is confined to a few blocks in all directions that are immediately adjacent to the premise that is being observed.

Primary objective is to select a suitable observation post or place for the surveillance.

If the area is rural, familiarity with the terrain and main highways as well as country roads is important. Nothing should be done to arouse curiosity in the neighborhood, or to get anyone to talk about the investigator's presence there. It is best not to make repeated trips throughout the neighborhood.

Please note that familiarizing oneself with the area is commonly done on the morning of the surveillance. We do not usually have the luxury of examining the area before the actual day of surveillance unless the investigator happens to be in the area. In most cases, it is not necessary to survey the area prior to the morning of the surveillance unless other information indicates different. Reality is that our clients do not want to pay for a special visit to the neighborhood to survey the situation unless it is warranted.

6. <u>Plan the Surveillance</u>

Some effort should be put forth in planning the surveillance such as whether the surveillance is going to be conducted by one investigator or more than one. If there is more than one investigator conducting the surveillance, then the investigators need to get together to go over strategy. The investigators must understand the procedures for the interchange of positions and under what situations or at what times the lead surveillance is changed. Organizational and procedural matters need to be settled, for example, the signal system should be perfected.

The investigator should plan to blend in with the environment in which the surveillance will be conducted. The type of clothing worn and the general appearance and behavior of the investigator should mesh with the area that he will be in so that nothing will appear conspicuous.

Foot surveillants should carry sufficient change for possible bus fares, taxi fares and other incidental costs that might arise while maintaining a continuous watch on the subject. Moving surveillants need to have money for gas and possible automotive emergencies, as well as for tolls and unexpected expenses.

In vehicular surveillance, changeable items of apparel are often carried to minimize recognition. These might include jackets, hats, caps, wigs, different types of eyeglasses, and other items that can be quickly changed. A foot surveillant may wear a jacket that can be reversed. In areas and seasons of frequent rain , it is best to carry a rain slicker to avoid appearing conspicuous walking the street in short sleeves in a downpour. Pens and a notebook should always be carried. Some surveillants carry pocket sized recorders for making notes.

7. <u>Equipment</u>

When conducting vehicle surveillance it is necessary for the investigator to carry all of his camera equipment.

All observation and photographic equipment should be planned and arranged for before the actual surveillance begins. In addition, every piece should be pre-tested by the investigator to make certain that it is in good working order before it is taken into the field. There is nothing more aggravating, more frustrating and more inexcusable than to miss photographic documentation of evidence because the camera will not function correctly on the spur of the moment, or because it is not loaded or because the investigator simply forgot to adequately charge the battery or pick up a tape.

II. OBSERVATION POSTS AND STATIONARY SURVEILLANCE

Stationary surveillance may be a temporary stake out or it may call for prolonged observation of a suspect or suspect's premises. In its briefest and simplest form, it may only be an investigator sitting in the shadows of a doorway or sitting in an automobile watching a place down the street. In its most elaborate form, it is a fully equipped observation post set up in an office building, hotel, apartment house or other location from which a clear view may be had of the subject premises and all its entrances and exits.

A. Selecting the Observation Post

The first step in selecting a suitable observation post is a preliminary survey of the area surrounding the place to be watched. This was mentioned previously, however, this section will cover the subject in more detail. As mentioned previously, such survey should consider the character of a neighborhood and its residents, the types of businesses and social outlets in the area, and specifically, the most logical location for the observation post.

Surveillance for observation post selected must provide the best view of the place, including all exits, as well as the best cover for the surveillants. The post should be out of sight of anyone who might be accidentally or intentionally looking at or watching the surveillants. It is best to have an indoor observation post, however, this is usually not the case. Ninety-five percent of our surveillance work is conducted from a vehicle. When conducting surveillances outdoors, inside a vehicle, the surveillants need to find some sort of outdoor cover created by nature or man or operate in an area under some suitable community disguise.

Surveillants should have a reasonable cover story to use whenever it becomes necessary to make an explanation of their presence in the area. The true reason for their being in the area and the identity of the subject premise should never be disclosed to anyone. This includes the subject, business friends, neighbors or social acquaintances. Once the surveillance is completed, no one in the area should have knowledge of the subject premises. Obviously, if the surveillant is in the neighborhood for a few days or even one full day, some suspicion will be aroused on the part of the neighbors, however, it should be those neighbors that are at least one block away from the subject premises and who are less likely to have any dealings with the subject. The secrecy during a surveillance must be maintained.

1. Surveillant Movements

The secrecy of the surveillance depends not only on the extent of the undercover protection provided by the observation post, but also the actions of the surveillants themselves. All movements to and from the post should be routine and as noticeable as possible. In no way should the surveillants attract attention to themselves. Surveillants should be especially careful not to arouse suspicious when they:

1. Establish the observation post.
2. Come and go to and from the post.
3. Leave the post to terminate the surveillance.

Every precaution should be taken when performing any activity that may be observed by others so that the surveillants can remain unsuspected and incognito.

2. Equipment

During all surveillances, the surveillant should be fully equipped in reference to video equipment. The equipment is fairly bulky and should always be kept out of sight of anyone passing by the surveillance position. This can be accomplished by keeping the equipment in cases covered by a towel. Not only should the video equipment be kept covered, but also any notes pertaining to the case. It is not unusual to be on a surveillance and have someone walk up to you surveillance vehicle and start a conversation. If papers are left lying around in a car, they can be easily viewed by others.

3. Indoor Observations Posts

Indoor surveillance enables the surveillant to remain undercover and to set up their equipment and conduct their operation out of view of passers by and persons who may be frequenting the premises under surveillance.

Inside the observation rooms, the surveillants should take positions several feet away from the windows. They should never stand or sit near a window. They should not be observed through the window from the street below or from offices or rooms across the street.

As far as possible, the investigator should eliminate the chances of curious people somehow peering through the glass into their post. Window draperies can be partially drawn and blinds can be pulled completely down to within a few inches of the windowsill. Observations can be made from above or below the window shade, or from a small opening in the drawn draperies.

4. Outdoor Surveillance Post

As in most cases, indoor surveillance positions are not available and therefore must be conducted outdoors. Surveillants have to find some sort of outdoor cover created by nature or man, conduct their surveillance from an equipped vehicle, or operate in the open under some suitable community disguise.

The nature, extent and duration of the surveillance will affect the type of outdoor role assumed by the investigator.

Surveillances conducted by our agency are usually conducted from an automobile. It is best to select several viewing points, if possible, so that the surveillant can move from time to time and is never in one place for a prolonged period of time. This is not always possible, and in some cases it is best to stay in one position if there is good cover. Discretion must be used in this area.

When conducting stationary surveillance from an automobile, the following are effective guidelines:

1. Never park in the same block as the place to be watched. The next block is the closest that an investigator should get to the subject's place.

2. Always drive to and from the position in a normal manner, like one of the residents of the area.

3. When moving form one vantage point to another, do so as inconspicuously as possible without any unusual activity.

4. After parking the car the surveillant should sit in the passenger seat rather than the driver seat. It will appear as though the surveillant is waiting for the driver.

5. An alternative to the above is to have the surveillant sit in the back seat, lower the sun visors, raise the headrests and put up a sun shade to make the surveillant's presence less easily detected. The sun shields that stretch across the front windows serve as a good cover in appropriate situations. A coat or shirt on the hanger in the back seat can also help a great deal.

6. Always use a car that is inconspicuous in make or color (like Magnum's red Ferrari, right!) and one that is so average that it will not draw attention to itself or to its occupants. The vehicle should be parked out of site in a position so that it is not in direct view of anyone that may be peering through the subject's windows or in the direct view of any close neighbors. More importantly, the surveillant should

not be visible to anyone at the subject's residence or close neighbors.

7. When it is necessary to park along side the road in front of a residence, park between two properties so that either resident doesn't feel as though they are being watched or that you are on their property.

Vans are effective observation posts. Various methods have been used to camouflage vans to hide the surveillance observations.

Some vans use one-way glass through which observations can be made; other use curtains that are partially drawn. Others have the appearance of a delivery truck with boxes stacked inside equipped with camouflage peepholes.

Some investigators follow the practice of getting people accustomed to the presence of the van by driving it to the area and leaving it there part of the day several days before starting actual surveillance. Each morning the driver locks the van and leaves to return later in the day. On the morning the surveillance begins, he drives as usual to the viewing site, parks the van, locks the surveillants and their equipment hidden inside.

As with the automobile, the van should be positioned so that it is partially hidden from the view of anyone at the subject's place.

5. <u>Surveillance, Rural Areas</u>

Trees are among the most useful natural covers: Large bushes, brush piles, tree stumps and the like provide suitable cover. Nature provides other possible surveillance points in its rock formations, ravines, gullies, crops, hillside brush, and similar cover.

Surveillants can also take advantage of manmade or man provided barriers to help to hide them from easy view. Fences and outdoor equipment for example can help hide at least part of the human body or the automobile.

Whether a surveillant should move into his rural observation post on foot or in some sort of vehicle depends on such factors as:

1. The kind of natural cover provided by the area.
2. The extent of large open spaces to be crossed.
3. The need to avoid the curiosity of residents of the area.
4. Importance of being able to return to the vehicle quickly.
5. The importance of keeping the subject premise under direct observation as opposed to a block or two away.

When the surveillant finds it necessary to move in and out of a site on foot, he should:

1. Avoid regularly used footpaths where he is more likely to meet other persons. They may realize he is a stranger in the area and wonder why he is there.

2. Always try to keep some object between yourself and the subject's premises. By doing so, you create a blind spot for anyone who might look your way, trees, clumps of bushes, straw stacks or haystacks, farm equipment, stone piles, etc., can be used. Any one of these objects between the investigator and the subject's premises will reduce the likelihood of the investigator being seen, as he will naturally focus in on the closer objects.

3. Walk on hard surfaces as far as possible. Hard surfaces do not leave footprints, but soft surfaces do. Certain surfaces are noisy by nature and must be walked over with greater care.

4. Always walk quietly and unhurriedly. An investigator should never rush in or out of an observation post.

5. Pause frequently to look around discreetly and listen carefully for sounds and movement.

6. Always walk below the crest of a hill.

7. As far as possible, avoid crossing large open spaces.

8. When possible, walk into the wind or across the wind. This tactic makes it more difficult for dogs to pick up an investigator's scent. It is usually better to try to quiet an approaching dog and make friends with it rather than create the added commotion of trying to scare it away.

9. Use a somewhat different route each time when entering the observation post. Do not create a pathway that can be used as others by a tracking method.

10. If possible, move into the observation post at night under the cover of darkness. When traveling during the daylight hours, schedule comings and goings at different times so as not to create a regular time schedule for the investigator's activities in the area. Also, coordinate traveling time when there is less activity in the subject's neighborhood.

11. When leaving the post, the investigator should make certain that he has left nothing behind that would create a suspicion of surveillance or identify the investigator.

III. AUTOMOBILE SURVEILLANCE

A moving surveillance, a tail or shadow, may be on foot, in a vehicle, or may use a combination of walking and riding.

B. Selecting Surveillance Vehicles

1. Surveillants should avoid attaching any features to surveillance vehicles that would attract attention to them. There should be no observable distinguishing features or decorations, outside or inside the cars that could attract the attention of other motorists or pedestrians. This includes no decorations of any sort on the hood, wheels, bumper, or windshield. No bumper stickers, fancy wheel covers, or attention attracting objects dangling form the rear view mirror. The only exception would be objects or stickers that are used to alter the appearance of the surveillance vehicle while the surveillance is in progress.

2. All surveillant vehicles should be in excellent operating condition. They should be kept tuned, filled with gas, and the ignition system should be working at optimum level. The cars must be capable of any quick maneuver and set for any road condition.

C. Conducting Surveillance

It is important to know that rear vision views often have blind spots, which means there are areas behind the subject's car where it is more difficult for him to get a good look at who may be following him. Cars with two side mirrors have better rear vision than those with only one. The best place for the surveillant car to drive is to the right and behind the subject with another car between,. The lane to the subject's right usually falls within his greater rear vision blind spot. Blind spots are located outside the view area covered by the rear vision mirror and the left side mirror. On a three-lane street with the subject's car in the middle lane, the blind spots would be the right land and part of the left inside lane. The subject's best view is of traffic in the lane directly behind him, with a partial view of the lane to his left. Blind spots should be taken advantage of whenever possible when tailing another vehicle, and also when the investigator approaches an occupied parked vehicle on foot.

As in all surveillance situations, the two primary risks are being detected and losing the subject. The closer one is to the subject, the greater the detection risk. The farther one is from the subject, the greater the risk of losing him. To achieve the delicate balance between the two calls for considerable driving skill.

The driver must stay close enough to keep the subject in view.

As mentioned previously, when following someone for a long period of time, it is advisable to change disguises. Elaborate disguises are not recommended. Simple disguises such as putting on or taking off a cap, hat or wig, or changing sunglasses is advisable.

Some investigators carry items that can be used to make the interior of a car appear different. These changes can all be made while the subject is turning a corner or during any time when the surveillant car is not within view of the subject's car.

1. Initiating Surveillance

During the preliminary survey, the surveillant selects a good starting point, a position of advantage from which they can watch and wait for the subject to appear.

The traffic in the area affects the location of the surveillance position. If it is an area of reasonably heavy traffic it can be closer to the subject's place. If it is an area of very little traffic the surveillant's car must be located at a greater distance from the subject's place because movement in the area will be more readily noticeable and identifiable. In such instances it is best to have a pair of binoculars available so that the surveillant can be certain it is the subject entering and leaving in his car and not someone else. Also, when starting out it is best to determine the most likely route that the subject would take on leaving the residence and take up a surveillance position accordingly. It is best to take up a position where the subject is less likely to pass by the surveillant.

If the subject travels towards the surveillant vehicle then the investigator must react quickly by slumping down in the vehicle to avoid being detected. A window open an inch or two will greatly help you hear the cars go by. The best alternative is to leave the surveillance position quickly to a position where the subject's vehicle can be observed. Pulling into a driveway, parking lot or other location can reduce the chances of the subject taking notice to the investigator's vehicle or the investigator. Look for such turn around spots <u>before</u> starting the surveillance.

When the surveillant is sitting in his vehicle, it is important to watch for close neighbors passing by or neighbors on foot or bicycle. The same maneuvers should be made as mentioned above. It is essential that the surveillant avoid being noticed by the subject, the subject's family or any close neighbors.

It is also important for the surveillant to keep in mind that anyone leaving the subject's residence or close neighbors could return to the neighborhood at any time. If at all possible the surveillant should attempt to make himself and his vehicle less noticeable.

2. <u>Techniques of Vehicle Surveillance (Surveillance Do's)</u>

For speedy reference, techniques of vehicle surveillance are as follows:

1. The surveillant's vehicle, usually an automobile but perhaps a van or truck should blend naturally with the vehicular traffic of the area. Its model, make and color should be inconspicuous.

2. When more than one surveillance car is used each should be of a different color and make.

3. Drivers should alter their driving techniques from time to time but should generally take advantage of the subject's rear vision blind spots. They should try to make it difficult for the subject to observe the surveillant's car(s) while at the same time keeping the subject's car in view. Surveillants' cars must be driven by drivers with quick reflexes who can think and act on the spur of the moment.

4. If there are two surveillants in the vehicle one should drive and watch the traffic and the other should watch the subject's car. The observer can also keep the surveillance log and function as the jumper should temporary foot surveillance be required.

5. Automobile surveillants should drive normally and blend in with the flow of traffic. They must avoid quick spurts of speed and if they need to speed up do so gradually. They should try to abstain from running red lights in pursuit and from other irregular moves that attract attention. It often requires considerable skill to negotiate traffic and keep the surveillance from becoming obvious.

6. In vehicular surveillance a man and a woman in a car would usually arouse less suspicion than two men.

7. Distance behind the subject's car is always a key factor. It varies according to circumstances. It would be less in crowded city traffic and greater on the highways and in rural areas. On downtown streets, in large cities, the usual procedure is to keep one car, not more than two cars between the subject's car and the surveillant's vehicle. In residential areas, the surveillant vehicle should stay at least one block behind the subject's vehicle. In rural areas, distances are increased as necessary, but the investigator must always keep within sight range.

8. When using two vehicles the most usual driving position is for the lead car to follow the subject car one or two cars behind it and in the lane to the right of it, unless the subject's car is already in the right lane, in which case the lead car follows behind it. The backup car would follow approximately

the same distance behind the lead car in the left lane. These cars can readily change positions in the normal flow of traffic by the lead car slowing down and the backup car speeding up a bit to take over the lead position, each of the cars moving into their respective lanes.

9. When there is only one investigator in the vehicle, the investigator has to watch the street traffic, pedestrians, and the subject's car all at the same time. It is important for the surveillant to be familiar with the appearance of the subject's vehicle form behind as well as the subject so that both can be quickly spotted if surveillance contact is broken for a period of time.

10. When it is a one-vehicle surveillance it is best for the surveillant to stay in the lane to the right of the subject to make it more difficult for the subject to see the investigator. If the subject is in the right curb lane and the car between moves out of that lane to the left, the surveillant can move into the left lane also. If there are three lanes, the investigator may prefer the middle lane so that he can negotiate a move to the right or left should the subject's car turn in either direction. Positioning of the surveillant's car is always a matter of good common sense and judgment in the light of all prevailing conditions.

11. When the subject is stopped at a red light and is in the right lane of traffic the investigator should keep in mind that the subject could make a right turn. If the investigator is one vehicle behind the subject he may be left sitting in the right lane of traffic due to the vehicle in front of him having elected to go straight instead of right.

12. It's important for the investigator to maintain visual contact of the subject's vehicle at all times if possible. Don't let the surveillance become routine, even on a turnpike or interstate. It is very easy for the investigator to lose sight of the subject in traffic if the investigator's attention is elsewhere.

13. When the subject leaves it is very important that you waste no time in getting on him. The most likely time that you will lose the subject is in the beginning. With that in mind, watch his taillights for when he steps on the brakes to shift the car into reverse or drive. Backup lights should be watched. Exhaust can often be a good indication that the car has been started. Keep the motor vehicle in view when it is parked at the subject's home whenever possible.

14. Always be looking ahead. Look for upcoming stop signs, cautions signs, curves, the timing of stoplights. Keep an eye on the subject's directional if he uses them and keep a mental map in your mind of the general direction that the subject appears to be going.

15. When traveling on an interstate or turnpike, surveillance should be tightened up when exits are coming up and loosened up when exits are some distance away. Always prefer the right hand side since to get off the highway the subject will have to take the right hand lane with very few exceptions.

16. When the subject stops at a light, stop sign, or in traffic, the normal distance whether you are following someone or not is to have the license plate of the vehicle in front resting on the top of your hood. When you have stopped, this is the normal distance to wait behind the other person. Any closer or further is abnormal and will attract some attention.

17. Do not let more than two cars come between you in city traffic. Avoid allowing vans, buses, trucks and pedestrians come in front of you. Try to evaluate the driver that is trying to come in between you.

18. When you enter the highway behind a subject check you watch immediately when the subjects heads onto the ramp. Calculate in your mind what delay has been made from the time that the subject entered the ramp to that point in time that you finally got on. This is extremely important since the distance that the subject will gain on you is incredible once he gets on the highway. For example, if the subject is forty-five seconds ahead of you and travels sixty miles per hour, the subject will gain three-quarters of a mile in the time it takes you to enter the highway. You would then travel seventy miles per hour for four and a half minutes' time (or about five and a half miles) just to catch up to the subject. Needless to say this means that you should avoid any excess delays in following the individual onto the highway, but when it occurs expect to do some driving before you see the subject again.

    If it is forty miles to the next exit you have nothing to worry about, but if the exits are only a couple of miles apart you can be in serious trouble with even a half-minute delay.

19. Be aware of the general direction in which the subject appears to be traveling. For example, if the subject is traveling in a general northeasterly direction and you lose him, you may come to a fork in the road where the choice is northeast or northwest. Obviously, you take the northeast direction.

20. Remember that people do not usually go very far from their home. People seldom go more than a couple of miles from home, so if you lose them check the area where they were last seen. Don't go off onto a highway and travel for an hour's ride expecting to pick up on the subject. Stay where you lost the subject and check that area with extreme care. Ninety percent of the time you will relocate the subject. Make sure the check is systematic. After checking the area return to the subject's house or other

likely locations that were identified through surveillance up to that point or on a previous occasion.

21. Do not get overly nervous when following a subject. This will eventually take its toll on your alertness and abilities to stay with the subject. If you go into a surveillance with the attitude you are going to be "made" you eventually will be, or you will lose the subject. Do not go into a surveillance with the attitude that if you lose the subject you can "get the subject another day". Even though this is true, it is a waste of the investigator's time and the client's money. As your experience grows you will find that you seldom, if ever, lose anyone and most of the times that you did lose a subject it was because of your own self-consciousness. <u>When confronted with a choice to either stay on a subject or possibly attract attention, or loosen up and possibly lose the subject, take the choice of staying with the subject.</u>

22. In business areas when the subject enters an establishment or home for any length of time and you have to remain in the area and you are on foot, try to get off the sidewalk and wait in hallways of office buildings or apartment houses, etc. Look through the front door and thereby attract no attention from any passersby except people entering or leaving the building. Have a good excuse ready for hanging around, be it for the benefit of the tenants or anyone else. Indicate that you are "waiting for a girlfriend" or grab a paper bag filled with trash, which might look like a lunch bag and indicate that you are waiting for a ride to a new job.

23. When there is a school crossing guard or other live obstruction anywhere near where you are taking a subject out of an area on a surveillance, it is sometimes smart to approach that person, explain your problem, and ask for their cooperation in letting you pass quickly when you leave. Most school crossing guards and security guards will cooperate with you and try to help if they know what you are doing.

    Needless to say, you never tell them or anyone else exactly who you are watching or why.

    3. <u>Surveillance Don'ts</u>

1. Don't be afraid that you are going to get "made" by the subject. Without exception every beginner doing surveillance makes this mistake and loses people because he thinks he has been made. Although you are important and very noticeable to yourself, you are just another face in the crowds to everyone else and if you dress normally, drive normal and look reasonably normal you should never have any problems.

2. Don't try to second-guess what the subject is doing. It is absolutely impossible to try to explain why people go where they go, do what they do,

etc. Avoid thinking about why the subject is making particular movements and avoid thinking that the subject's activities are affected by your presence. Merely follow the subject, note what the subject does, where they go, and try to figure it out later on.

3. Don't travel all over the world. If you have lost someone, proceed immediately in that general direction that you last saw them headed and after you have exhausted that possibility reasonably, stop, and turn back. Then check the immediate area in which they were lost. If you do not find them go back to the last place that they were seen, their house, or any other location that you suspect they may have gone to within reason, based on earlier surveillance reports or background knowledge. Do not travel long distances hoping to get "lucky" because you will not. If you are unable to find them return to their house and await their return. Get the best vantage possible for the most absolute best film. When they return home and have dozens of brown plastic bags in the trunk of their car saying "Wal-Mart" there's no longer any doubt where they had gone. Our goal now is to get the best video of them unloading the car to document their physical capabilities of bending over, lifting and carrying heavy bags of groceries in each hand.

4. Don't forget that three pictures are necessary in a person's mind to begin to become suspicious of you. This means that the subject must have three good, clear, lasting looks at your face before they become suspicious that you are following them or that they're running into you too often. This doesn't mean passing glances while you are driving by at thirty miles per hours in a car and they merely look at the vehicle. This means three good full looks at you where your face registers. After you have had two of these happen to you where the subject just looks at your face, etc., try to delay the third one happening as long as possible, or change your appearance, vehicle, etc., before that third picture is taken in their mind. At that point, if you're relatively certain that you've been "made" discontinue and come back at a later date.

5. Don't check in with the police department unless necessary. Do not broadcast to the police or other officials that you are conducting surveillance in that certain area unless you feel that it is absolutely necessary. The less people that know about your activity, the better, and if something does go wrong you will not be blaming the police unfairly just because you checked in with them.

6. Don't get ahead of the subject. Never pass the subject's vehicle or pass him on foot unless it is absolutely necessary. This is a terrible mistake to make and a very bad habit to get into, which will cause you many wasted hours.

7. Don't leave your car unless absolutely necessary. If you do have to leave your automobile make sure you are able to get back to the automobile before the subject leaves in his vehicle. Many times an investigator will be caught too far away from his vehicle and the subject drives out of sight. The investigator should leave his surveillance position only when he is relatively certain that the subject will not be leaving the area or when he knows that he will be able to return to his vehicle in time to follow the subject.

8. Never throw trash from your car when sitting on a surveillance. If you are questioned by the police and they see such a mess they will not be convinced that you are a professional and to be taken seriously. This may seem like a small point but you need all the goodwill you can get and littering is no way to get it.

9. Don't get into an interesting book or other reading material when you are on a surveillance. The next thing you know, three minutes have gone by and during the time the subject has left. Try the radio and various am and fm radio stations so as not to get bored.

V. DAILY SURVEILLANCE CHECK LIST

A. Preliminary Surveillance Investigation

Prior to arriving in the area, you should have already printed out your database background report. I usually run this and review it the night before my surveillance. I would have also used Google Earth to see if I can actually see a picture of my targets house. If a picture is not available there, I will check with the County Property Appraiser's Office on line as they also sometimes have a picture of the house. This search also verifies who owns the house and what the value of the house is. A value of a house can tell you a lot about the neighborhood and what to expect.

B. Arrival, Subject's Residence

On an initial surveillance assignment I will routinely arrive at 6:00 a.m. on a weekday and 7:00 a.m. on a weekend day.

Once I arrive in the neighborhood, I will look to see if I see the cars identified in the database I reviewed. This will be the first indicator that my subject still lives at the reported address.

C. Canvass Neighborhood

I will circle the area to look for the exits so that I don't get caught off guard when they leave the area. I should have a general idea of which way they will depart and which way leads to the closest store or business area.

D. Take up Surveillance Position

The surveillance position you choose will be the most important decision you make and could make or break the investigation. Too far away and you risk missing activity, too close and you risk being spotted.

1. As a rule of thumb, the subject's front door and or car and driveway should be observable form your position. You need to see if they are picked up by someone else, leave on foot or leave in their personal vehicle. '
2. I prefer to have my car pointed away from the subject's residence and off to a wide peripheral spot usually affording some obstruction of my car.

E. Observations
1. My first notes in the case will be a complete description of the house and cars and any special characteristics which make my subjects house stand out or seem pertinent to the case.
2. I will continue to make hourly notations throughout the day until my subject moves then those notations become specific to my subject, where they went and how they moved in reference to their reported injury.

Chapter Eight
Private Investigator Equipment

I. Basic knowledge of specialty investigation equipment.
II. Basic knowledge on the proper\legal use of audio recorder/audio recording.
III. Basic knowledge on the proper\legal use of video recorders/video recording.
IV. Basic knowledge on the proper\legal use of still cameras\still photography.
V. Understand when to use photography on surveillance.

8. Equipment For the Professional Investigator

One of the most important objectives of any surveillance is to obtain video of your subject. As a rule of thumb, you should know that any video taken of your subject during surveillance which has an elapsed time of less than ten or fifteen minutes of your subject's activities will, for the most part, be considered inadequate for most investigative purposes. The first thing we should talk about is the use of your camcorder. When you're videoing, you must train your camera on the subject of your investigation and leave it there. Taking fifteen minutes of video during the course of your investigation, ten minutes of which is nothing but your subject's home or car will never be sufficient. In surveillance, it's important to remember that your goal is to objectively document your subject's movement and behavior through the use of video. That means obtaining video of the activities your subject is engaged in. Video of residences, vehicles or persons not directly pertinent to your investigation will not be of any help to you. It's up to you as a professional private investigator to take this untrained video camera and teach it to perform to your specifications by recoding the subject under surveillance.

Video cameras have come a long way and I can recall the early days when the video recorder was a reel to reel machine with an attached camera on a cord. Cameras especially surveillance cameras, were two—piece units where the camera was separate from the actual recording device. Of course, this situation created a cumbersome problem in that the moving of the two individual pieces, which were connected by a cable, was not only a difficult job but extremely conspicuous when used in the field situation. With the introduction of the one piece camera and recorder combination called the "camcorder", the ability to conceal your video camera was increased tremendously. The camcorder is readily concealable and extremely portable so it can be used in a variety of hidden applications. Today, microchip technology has created pin hole cameras that enable covert videoing on flash cards or mini hard drives half the size of a pack of cigarettes. Considering their size the options that you have in concealing such units are almost limitless. Companies like Super Circuits out of Texas, have the ability to hide a surveillance camera in a clock, radio, fire alarm, emergency light systems, stereos, books, briefcases, garbage cans, fence posts, power transformers, picture frames, loose—leaf binders, lamps, radar detectors and even mailboxes. Some organizations even specialize in hiding video cameras in stuffed animals. Because of advanced chip technology and the miniaturization of the video camera, or surveillance camera, the possibilities for the concealment of your camcorder are almost limitless.

As a private investigator, your camera is your weapon. You must be comfortable and knowledgeable in its use and applications. Practice shooting video by going to a busy shopping center or grocery store and video people coming and going form their car to the front door and from the front door to their car. Most camcorders are also equipped with a red, flashing LED light mounted on the front of the camcorder. This light called the "tally light" and can be turned off in the camera settings mode. If it cannot be turned off you will want to put a small piece of black electrical tape and cover the LED light on the front of your camcorder before conducting any surveillance investigation. This, once again, will allow you to video your subject without anyone around you being aware of the fact that you're recording their movements. Before utilizing your camcorder or any advanced video surveillance equipment, we strongly recommend that you read, in detail, the instructions accompanying the equipment. Once again, it is important that you familiarize yourself with any video surveillance equipment before ever attempting to utilize it in the field. Your comfort level with this equipment is fundamental to your success in the field as an investigator. Practice, practice, practice.

The stock camera battery can always be upgraded with an extended life one a standard upgrade is a two hour battery. Remember to remove the battery from your camcorder during periods of inactivity when the camera is not in use. If you charge your battery to its full capacity the evening before conducting the surveillance and attach it to your camcorder, by the time you begin your surveillance the next morning, you could lose some of the battery's capacity. Remember, leave your battery unattached until you're ready to use it. Always have a second and maybe even a third fully charged battery as part of your accessories. You never know when you will may need to shoot a full day's activity so be prepared. Always bring your charger with you so that you can be recharging a battery while using another.

A professional private investigator will also want to invest in a camcorder cigarette lighter battery cord. In this manner, the camcorder can be operated via a cigarette lighter battery cord, using your automobile battery as your source for power. Your camcorder batteries can then be utilized when you leave your vehicle, giving you the maximum benefit of portability. Using your power sources in this manner will increase your effectiveness as an investigator in the field by prolonging your opportunities for video surveillance. Most cameras also serve as chargers now so with the cigarette battery cord, you can charge a battery in between shooting or carry a second camera of the same make and model, which is also highly recommended.

Never, use the automatic focus functions on your camcorder when filming. The automatic focus should be used before you actually film just to set the correct focus for the distance you are shooting. Once the auto focus is set, turn it OFF. This is important because the automatic focus function on your camcorder automatically focuses on the nearest object to the camcorder. This means that if a person or a motor vehicle, a leaf, a bush, a fly or even a speck of dust comes between you and the subject that you're attempting to video, the camcorder will refocus on this interference until it passes and then again attempt to refocus on your subject. Time and time again, valuable and irreplaceable video has been lost by professional investigators who become lackadaisical and forget to place their camcorder on manual focus or know how to turn it on and off quickly.

The quality of the lens your camera has is an extremely important part of your choice of which camera to purchase. Most camcorders come equipped with an 8:1 or 12:1 zoom capability. However, for surveillance situations, this won't allow you to get close enough to your subject in all cases. Look for a camera with at least a 22/1 optical zoom capacity. If you're attempting to take video from a distance of one or two blocks, or in some cases further than this, you may find it advantageous to utilize a telephoto lens. The telephoto lens will significantly multiply the effectiveness of your camera's inter telephoto optical capabilities. Using a telephoto lens also gives you the ability to distance yourself from the subject of your surveillance. The use of a camera with a standard 22/1 optical lens will effectively create a buffer or safety zone of around 100 yards during your surveillance. Never consider the Digital Zoom capability of a camera as we do not use Digital Zoom technology during surveillance. This technology merely takes the pixels of an image and enhances them electronically splitting them and filling in the pixels to make the image look larger, but the quality is greatly depleted. This poor quality image, coupled with the necessity of needing to stream it over the internet will make your efforts look more like a mosaic piece of art rather than a surveillance film. So remember, we NEVER use the digital zoom technology and shut this feature off in the main camera settings.

Your camera should also be equipped with a color view finder to make spotting the subject in a diverse background quicker. Many inexpensive cameras cut corners by having a black and white view finder since they expect the camera user to use the flip open screen. While we use both in surveillance, we use the view finder more as it enables the investigator to more quickly locate the subject and steady the image simultaneously using both hands and your head.

Finally your camera should come equipped with "image stabilization" technology. This cuts down on any minor movement caused by free holding the camera.

<u>Camera Make Model and Specifications</u>

3. Lens capacity with at least a 22/1 Optical Resolution.
4. Image Stabilizer
5. Color Viewfinder
6. Manual Focus Button

Tripods/Monopods

1. Standard six foot tripod
2. Standard Monopod
3. Jo Mount specialty equipment

    The tripod is another important piece of equipment. One of the most common complaints about surveillance videotape is the fact that it is often so shaky that the viewer is unable to clearly identify the subject of an investigation or the activity that the subject is engaged in. A tripod can help to alleviate shaky videotape. There are several factors that can cause shaky video. First, you may be taping your subject for an extended period of time, often as long as an hour or more. It's very difficult to hold a camcorder still for ten minutes, let alone an hour. A tripod or single pod extending from the base of your camera will allow you to take clear and steady video. Secondly, if you're conducting surveillance from your vehicle, make sure that you turn your engine off while taping. It won't always be comfortable without air conditioning, but the vibration caused by your engine will significantly and adversely affect your video recording. If for some reason, you don't have a tripod, it's very important to use good video technique. Shooting steady videotape can also be accomplished by using a rest, or supporting the camera with both hands. Both elbows should be parallel to each other and tucked towards the middle of your chest. By holding the camcorder in this manner, you're allowing your skeletal structure to support the weight of the camcorder, instead of your muscles and tendons. If you hold the camcorder with one hand, flaring your elbow out to the side, your arms will inevitably become tired and start to shake, especially when you're taping for long periods of time. Using the proper recording technique that we've discussed will allow you to obtain clear and steady videotape evidence in almost any situation. However, you should always have and use a tripod for any extended vide recording.

If you are still using an older style camera with videotapes, then one videotape should be used for each subject you are surveilling. Never attempt to obtain evidence for another investigation on the same tape. Don't ever reuse an old tape or attempt to tape over old video. The risk of getting an old contaminated tape caught in your camera is not worth the $5.00 cost of a new tape. It is also extremely dangerous to review the videotape of your subject and then continue to use the same tape on a subsequent day. It's dangerous because most camcorders will automatically cut out a portion of the video when reactivated after playback. You may erase or lose valuable evidence by doing this.

    Remember that the camcorder is one of the professional investigator's most important pieces of equipment. Cameras have come down in costs tremendously but are still an investment and need to be taken care of properly. Your camcorder will be affected by moisture, extreme heat, extreme cold and sudden temperature changes. Therefore, your camcorder should never be left in your vehicle in the sun and heat for the entire day. Treat it like your pet — it'll die if improperly cared for or subjected to abuse and neglect. Never ever leave your camcorder in your vehicle overnight. Your vehicle is never a safe or secure place to leave expensive equipment or valuable evidence.

Let's recap the operation of your camcorder.

1. Always charge your batteries before leaving the house and don't leave a battery in a camera which is not in use.

2. Know your camera before you attempt to use it in the field.

3. Always turn your camera to manual focus before filming.

4. Paranoia has no place in securing video. Remember that your camera is pre–trained to record dashboards, floorboards and trees. You must train your camera to stay on the subject under surveillance, no matter what happens, keep the subjects head at the top of your view finder screen and his feet at the bottom of your view finder screen.

5. Don't attempt to review your video in the field until your entire investigation is complete, so as to ensure no accidental erasure takes place.

GPS

When I initially started I recall doing investigations without a GPS. In fact for years I argued with my wife that I did not need a GPs because I had map quest on my phone and before that because I printed out directions to my surveillance or investigation prior to leaving the house. I just couldn't justify why I should pay money for a device I really didn't need. But I couldn't have been more incorrect, after almost three years of refusing the device, I received one from Santa. I didn't realize how much time I had wasted following a map or driving directions. And in those cases were I would go to one address and find my subject no longer lived there and then needed to follow-up visiting several other addresses the GPS was incredible of getting me from one location to the next. And even in surveillances when I was following someone on a day of errands and then entered their address as we headed back, I saw I could foresee all of the subject's turns. And then there were those cases when I thought the claimant was purposely taking me into a quiet residential area in order to detect a tail, but my GPS re-assured me this was a short cut back to the claimant's house. And then there are the special investigation days when I would set out to interview one person only to find this subject identified two more witnesses and just by calling them I could enter their address in my GPS and let the witness know exactly when I would be there to secure their statements.

I am now the GPS markets biggest advocate, it is a must have tool for the mobile investigator.

Equipment List

A. <u>Covert Camera</u>

1. Small Comfortable item with ability to hook in video capture device.
2. Button Camera with hard drive, preferable hard wired with viewing monitor.
3. Date and Time compatible
4. Reliable! No cheap Glasses, Pen Cameras

B. <u>Camouflage Clothing and Backpack</u>

1. Full gear obtainable from army navy store
2. Binoculars
3. Bug spray
4. Pruning clippers
5. Collapsible Stool
6. Tri –pod
7. Duct Tape

C. <u>Statement Recorder</u>

1. Hard drive USB
2. Ear bud Microphone for Two Way Statement Recording

D. <u>Lap Top</u>

1. With-in last three years model

D. <u>Smart Phone</u>

1. With internet service with e-mail set up
2. Notes Application

E. Pinnacle or Dazzle Video Capture

F. In-Car Cooling Unit- Swampy.net

There is only one cooler that will really work in the Florida heat and this is made by swamy.net. You can buy just the top part and use your own cooler. This the ONLY cooler I will recommend. The MK3 ($600) and MK4 ($650)

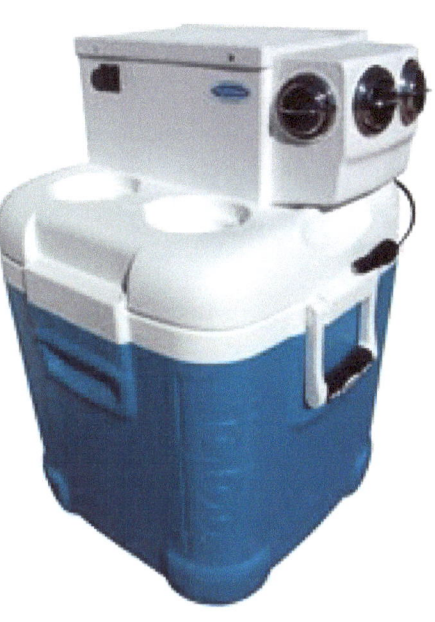

Chapter Nine
Safe Guarding and Restricted Information

I. Gramm-Leach-Bliley Act
II. Fair Credit Reporting
III. NCIC

Gramm–Leach–Bliley Act (GLB)

The Gram-Leach-Bliley Acr (GLB) also known as the Financial Services Modernization Act of 1999, (Pub.L. 106-102, 113 Stat. 1338, enacted November 12, 1999) is an act of the 106th United States Congress (1999–2001). It was signed into law by President Bill Clinton and it repealed part of the Glass-Steagall Act of 1933, opening up the market among banking companies, securities companies and insurance companies. The Glass-Steagall Act prohibited any one institution from acting as any combination of an investment bank, a commercial bank, and an insurance company.

The Gramm–Leach–Bliley Act allowed commercial banks, investment banks, securities firms, and insurance companies to consolidate. For example, Citicorp (a commercial bank holding company) merged with Travelers Group (an insurance company) in 1998 to form the conglomerate Citigroup, a corporation combining banking, securities and insurance services under a house of brands that included Citibank, Smith Barney, Primerica, and Travelers. This combination, announced in 1998, would have violated the Glass-Steagall Act and the Bank Holding Company Act of 1956 by combining securities, insurance, and banking, if not for a temporary waiver process. The law was passed to legalize these mergers on a permanent basis.

Changes Caused by the Act

Many of the largest banks, brokerages, and insurance companies desired the Act at the time. The justification was that individuals usually put more money into investments when the economy is doing well, but they put most of their money into savings accounts when the economy turns bad. With the new Act, they would be able to do both 'savings' and 'investment' at the same financial institution, which would be able to do well in both good and bad economic times.

What Does the GLB Act have to do With Being a PI?

With poeples personal information becoming more condensed and available at one location, the fear of Identity theft becomes more of a concern. Now a criminal may only have to access one major bank or insurance compnay and get personal information on thousands of account holders. So with the more ralxed fredoms GLB brough to businesses it alos brough a higher sence of securing the infomration busineses maintained. No longer could buisnesses sell your information without you authorizing or "Opting-In" to the sharing.

As a requirement for doing business under 493, Private Investigative Firms are to maintain investigative reports and records. These same reports could contain personal identifying information such as a person's date of birth, social security number and address. The same information, in the wrong hands could result in Identity Theft. Many large investigative agencies work with Insurance Companies who are specifically referenced in the GLB Act. They may be our clients and the information we have on file for a subject/target may have come directly from the Insurance Company. Therefore, it is crucial that the information and files a Private Investigations Firm maintains is held in a safe and secure manner.

Fair Credit Reporting Act (FCRA) is a United States Federal Law that regulates the collection, dissemination, and use of consumer information, including consumer credit information. Along with the Fair Debt Collection Practices Act (FDCPA), it forms the base of consumer credit rights in the United States.

Consumer Reporting Agencies

Consumer reporting agencies (CRAs) are entities that collect and disseminate information about consumers to be used for credit evaluation and certain other purposes, including employment. Credit bureaus, a type of consumer reporting agency, hold a consumer's credit report in their databases. CRAs have a number of responsibilities under FCRA, including the following:

1. Provide a consumer with information about him or her in the agency's files and to take steps to verify the accuracy of information disputed by a consumer.
2. If negative information is removed as a result of a consumer's dispute, it may not be reinserted without notifying the consumer within five days, in writing.
3. CRAs may not retain negative information for an excessive period (typically seven years from the date of the delinquency with the exception of bankruptcies (10 years) and tax liens (seven years from the time they are paid).

The three big CRAs — Experian, TransUnion, and Equifax — do not interact with information furnishers directly as a result of consumer disputes. They use a system called E-Oscar. In some areas of the country, however, there are other credit bureaus. For example, in Texas, if a consumer tries to dispute information with Equifax directly, they must go through CSC Credit Services which is linked to the Equifax database.

Nationwide Specialty Consumer Reporting Agencies

In addition to the three big CRAs, the FCRA also classifies dozens of other information technology companies as "nationwide specialty consumer reporting agencies" that produce individual consumer reports used to make credit determinations. Under Section 603(w) of the Fair Credit Reporting Act, the term "nationwide specialty consumer reporting agency" means a consumer reporting agency that compiles and maintains files on consumers on a nationwide basis relating to

1. medical records or payments;
2. residential or tenant history;
3. check writing history;
4. employment history; or
5. insurance claims.

Because these nationwide specialty consumer reporting agencies sell consumer credit report files, they are required to provide annual disclosures of their report files to any consumers who request disclosure. This list of compnaies includes some of the database compnaies investigative frms have access to like TLO who is owned by Trans Union, Insurance Services Office (ISO) which Insurance compnay claims prefessional use, Tenant Data Services and LexisNexis.

Any time an Investigative Firm as acccess to a specialty reporting agency, you will find that they have a subscriptuion agreement that requires vetting and strict access and use guidelines.

Likelihood of Errors on a Credit Report

A large portion of consumer credit reports contain errors. A study released by the U.S. Public Interest Research Group in June 2004 found that 79% of the consumer credit reports surveyed contained some kind of error or mistake. However, the General Accountability Office released a study disputing this figure but the fact remains that mistakes can happen and in the digital age this may be the result of an inaccurate reported Social Secuirty Number or addresss.

For the professinal PI, this means that the Database Reports we receive should used as an investigative tool only not factual information until verified by a seaparte and independent investigation.

III. **NCIC**

NCIC is a computerized index of criminal justice information (i.e.-criminal record history information, fugitives, stolen properties, missing persons). It is available to Federal, state, and local law enforcement and other criminal justice agencies and is operational 24 hours a day, 365 days a year.

It's been called the lifeline of law enforcement—an electronic clearinghouse of crime data that can be tapped into by virtually every criminal justice agency nationwide, 24 hours a day, 365 days a year.

The **National Crime Information Center**, or NCIC, was launched on January 27, 1967 and currently averages 7.5 million transactions per day.

NCIC helps criminal justice professionals apprehend fugitives, locate missing persons, recover stolen property, and identify terrorists. It also assists law enforcement officers in performing their official duties more safely and provides them with information necessary to aid in protecting the general public.

How NCIC is used: Criminal justice agencies enter records into NCIC that are accessible to law enforcement agencies nationwide. For example, a law enforcement officer can search NCIC during a traffic stop to determine if the vehicle in question is stolen or if the driver is a wanted by law enforcement. The system responds instantly. However, a positive response from NCIC is not probable cause for an officer to take action. NCIC policy requires the inquiring agency to make contact with the entering agency to verify the information is accurate and up-to-date. Once the record is confirmed, the inquiring agency may take action to arrest a fugitive, return a missing person, charge a subject with violation of a protection order, or recover stolen property.

The FBI provides a host computer and telecommunication lines to a single point of contact in each of the 50 states, the District of Columbia, Puerto Rico, the U.S. Virgin Islands, Guam, and Canada, as well as federal criminal justice agencies. Those jurisdictions, in turn, operate their own computer systems, providing access to nearly all local criminal justice agencies and authorized non-criminal justice agencies nationwide. The entry, modification, and removal of records are the responsibility of the agency that entered them.

Success Stories

Following a speeding-related traffic stop of an individual in Newhall, California in December 2005, the California Highway Patrol conducted a search of NCIC. The search produced a terrorism-related lookout instructing the officer to contact the FBI's Terrorist Screening Center (TSC) for assistance in identifying the subject, who was confirmed to be a positive identity match to the individual listed in the NCIC lookout and was the main subject of an FBI San Francisco international terrorism investigation. Traveling with the subject were two additional individuals who were fully identified. The subject was arrested for possession of methamphetamine, and a female passenger was arrested on two outstanding warrants.

In 2009, an NCIC search on a license plate number revealed the plate was linked to a vehicle owned by a man wanted for the July 2008 murder of his mother in Mississippi. When the Florida sheriffs that had queried the plate approached the vehicle, the suspect pulled a sawed-off shotgun from under a blanket and pointed the weapon at the deputies. The deputies shot and killed the suspect before he could fire.

Perhaps one of the more well-known examples of an NCIC search involved Oklahoma City bomber Timothy McVeigh.

After identifying McVeigh as the renter of the explosives-laden Ryder truck, investigators entered his name into the NCIC computer. About 90 minutes after the bombing, the Oklahoma State Highway Patrol made an inquiry on McVeigh. Armed with this information, investigators contacted the highway patrol and found that McVeigh was sitting—two days after the bombing—in a nearby jail cell on unrelated weapons charges.

NCIC searches are just another example of how Law Enforcement is leveraging technology and information-sharing to track down criminals.

MIS USE

Federal regulations and NCIC policy have classified NCIC information as <u>sensitive and have restricted access to and use of such information to authorized criminal justice agencies for criminal justice purposes.</u> These purposes include conducting criminal investigations or screening applicants for employment in criminal justice positions.

In December 1991, 20 individuals in New Jersey and Florida were indicted under federal bribery, theft of government property, and computer fraud statutes for selling criminal history information obtained from NCIC.

A private Investigator CAN NOT access this information. Asking your friend who is a Police Offcer to run apersons name through the NCIC database is a Felony!

Chapter Ten
Report Writing and Field Note Taking

- I. Introduction
- II. Adaptation of the Report
- III. Taking Notes
- IV. Using a Smart Phone
- V. Connecting the Dots
- VI. Proof Reading
- VII. Outline Samples
- VIII. Photos and Video Capture

10. Introduction

A report is the communication of information to others. The most important and essential ingredient of the report is "fact". Fact is generally described in reporting as "new information"

The ultimate basis of any good report is facts. That means direct observations, inspections, experience or research. By definition, a report must be more than vague "ideas" and "opinions". The ideas must have solid basis in fact.

The modern report is one of the most interesting developments of the last century. The growth of the technical professional in all industries and the widening activities of those responsible for handling concerns have all led to the increased need for written communication. Due to this extreme growth, the written report has become of utmost importance especially in providing a permanent record.

The report is an account of something heard, seen, read or done. A written report is an account of something heard, seen, read or done expressed in writing. In this day and time, reports play a large and important part of public and corporate affairs. If no standardized form is furnished, it is often very difficult to develop a logical arrangement for a report to incorporate all of the facts a good report must contain.

Adaptation to the Reader

A good report writer makes his reports fit the interests, peculiarities, knowledge and desires of his/her readers. No matter how correct the form of the report, the style is inadequate and poor if it is unsuited to the intended reader.

Therefore you do not want to be too overly technical. Attempt to relay your facts in clear, concise everyday language.

It is a very good idea to write down phrases that you will become accustomed to using often. Also the report, although factual, is more interesting if it tells a story and maintains a logical sequence of events in a commonsense sequence that the reader can follow. Your report should also attempt to answer any question it may present.

EXAMPLE
Upon my arrival at 5:30 a.m., I noticed the gate was open. According to the neighbor I spoke to later, I learned the subject usually leaves the gate open after she leaves in the morning and does not close it until she returns home in the evening.

Be Thorough

All of the facts that have a bearing on the incident must be recorded in an easy-to-read format. All directly connected circumstances must be included and addressed. Include all persons interviewed and steps taken. Remember your memory alone is not sufficient to insure completeness. You will have to refer to your filed notes, sketches, pictures, etc. If your report requires any further explanation, then you have not thoroughly answered the questions who, what where, when, why and how.

Be Accurate

One of the main requirements of a report is that it be accurate. Report on the facts of the incident. If opinions are reported, they must be clearly labeled as such. The information upon which a report is based must be factual.

Taking Notes

The heart of the report starts with good notes. Eventually you will learn quickly what types of notes you will need to compile a good report. By following your investigative outlines, you will not only learn ideas valuable in the investigation, but also to acquire and conduct the steps that would be expected.

These field notes are referred to as work product. They are usually the only notes used in testifying in a case. Your report written later is not considered work product and therefore often not admissible as evidence. If you can remember the O. J. Simpson trial you may recall the investigator who appeared on the stand flipping through his loose leaf book filled with his progressive field notes. These were the only notes he used to refresh his recollection of what he heard, saw, read or did at the time.

The better your notes are, the easier the report is to compile when you are done. And fortunately for all investigators the reporting process gets easier over time.

Use Your Smart Phone note Taking Application

After many years in business, I can say I have learned one thing, which is that I never stop learning. Learn to be a good listener as ideas will come to you if you are paying attention.

Recently, I had a grad student ask me, "if you could improve any part of your business what would it be?" I said, getting the investigators to spend less time procrastinating about their reports and just getting them in quicker. The sooner I get their investigative reports in the office, the quicker I can bill out their time and get our money. Cash flow is a big part of any business and your clients need to have their reports before they submit an invoice for payment. Even worse is to have ten investigators turn in nothing one week and then each of them turn in ten reports the following week making the fluctuation in work unpredictable and overwhelming. Getting my investigators to routinely turn in five completed reports a week on a steady basis would not only create a constant stream of income, but also a predictable work load. No investigative owner should ever assume he won't have to review reports. All reports must be reviewed by the owner or manager of the agency, no matter what the skill level of the case investigator may be.

After explaining my business in more depth, the grad student asked if I had considered offering incentives to the investigators. Why should I have to give an investigator an incentive or reward for doing his/her job. I explained that I had in the past gone this route through a program that rewarded the investigators with the highest bill-outs each week. I also paid a bonus to the investigator who shot the most video each month. Having been this route before, I now preferred a tool rather than a stimulus. I had used in the past dictation machines and voice recognition software which helped, but still required a lap top or significant editing. The grad student asked me if there was any one investigator that seemed to be more productive or turned in his work more regularity than the others and there was. By interviewing this person, we found that he would text message his notes throughout the day and email them to himself so that most of the report writing work was already done by the end of his day. Today, I encourage all investigators to use a notes application on their smart phone throughout the day to increase their productivity and reduce report writing time. As a result, I get constant case volume flow and constant weekly bill-outs. Investigators should have five days to work an assignment and be able to submit their report to the office within two days after working the case. There are plenty of investigators meeting these deadlines so encourage your investigators to meet these same standards.

Connecting the Dots

What I am going to say next may go against everything else you have ever heard about report writing. It may even go against prior training you have had as a Police Officer, Military Investigator or Detective. Since many Investigators come from a law enforcement environment, they are routinely told to keep their opinions out of a report and report just the facts. It is typically a supervisor or prosecuting attorney that analyzes your information and develops a legal strategy. However in the private sector, there is only you and your client. In a domestic case, you are the professional who needs to thoroughly explain the value of the evidence you developed. In an insurance case, the claim investigator needs to lead the adjuster through the investigation so important evidence can be gathered for the defense. Think of it this way, an attorney will take a case and in a court room setting deliver an opening argument. The argument will be what they think happened and how they intent to prove it or what the other party contends and how they intend to rebut it. This is where they add their strategy and then begin to submit the evidence to make their argument. A good PI, based on his experience will usually have a plan of action in mind or develop a plan once some information has been developed. The bottom line is that in order to be valuable to our client we need to serve their interests. This means develop information helpful to the reason we were hired.

Whether you like it or not, you are not impartial, you work for your client and are looking to develop information helpful to them not information detrimental to them. This is the business side of being a private investigator. You need to understand that it's not just reporting the facts regardless of what they are. It is your job to interpret your findings and report then in the best light and most favorable light of your client. Throughout your report you need to keep in mind your position and strategy. The Private Investigator hired by OJ Simpson did not look for evidence that pointed to him being guilty. He was developing information to show or imply his innocence.

If my client was reported to have selfishly drank the last of the water in a survivor situation, after my investigation I may write that my investigation learned that the glass of water was left half full. I don't want to give the connotation it was half empty and in fact I may have even learned or secured a statement saying that the glass was never filled to the top. So I present a problem for my accuser in determining exactly how much my client even ever drank. Maybe it was just a sip and it was predetermined that everyone could take a sip each day so my client did nothing wrong. In this simple exercise, I developed a defense once I learned a little about the details. This is the same exercise you must go through with each and every case you work. Your efforts regardless of how they were preformed must be interpreted and reported in a manner beneficial to your client.   Sometimes you will need to lake extra steps to prove your point.

Proofreading

After you have completed your report, you should read your report thoroughly to make sure that it says exactly what you desire it to say. A good report writer will be totally objective while proofreading his report; try to imagine yourself as the reader and not the writer. Look for essential things that you may have over looked in the report. Read your report out loud. Awkward phrasing is often hard to read orally. By doing this you should get some idea of how effectively you organize your thoughts.   And by all means spellcheck your reports.

Reporting and Investigations Outline Samples

Many Companies have specific reports formats they will require you to follow. The following report formats are just an example or recommendation of a report format. It is important that each investigator be completely familiar with report styles and rules for reporting. It is very important to keep to a format so that all reports conform to a particular flow. This way your clients will get use to where to look for specific information and can resource it quickly when needed.

Follow your report outline as close as possible so as not to leave out any information. Review not only your outline but also <u>any particular requests made by the client</u>. Review any information given to you by the client or by your company. Typically at the onset of an assignment you will receive specific instructions specifying your assignment. This assignment sheet must be carefully and thoroughly reviewed so that all of your client's questions and pertinent information are covered in your report and the report is <u>adapted</u> to your client's interests and concerns. A good report format can keep you on track and emphasize your ability to provide a results oriented product. The following is just an example and not meant to be the best or only option. Your agency will provide you with a report sample to follow. If you are staring out on your own, it is recommended that you design your own report formats and outlines to follow and keep your reports consistent looking. I have provided an example of a surveillance outline report for your review.

CONFIDENTIAL INVESTIGATIVE REPORT
(DATE)

CLIENTS COMPANY	Re:	Your File No. : 000-00-000
CLIENT'S NAME		Addt'l File No. : 0000-00000
STREET ADDRESS		Our File No. : 000-0000-000
CITY, STATE, ZIP, CODE		Insured: NAME OF INSURED
		Employee: NAME OF EMPLOYEE
		SSN: (Partial)
		D/L: DATE OF LOSS

Assignment Received	:	MONTH/DAY/YEAR
Previous Correspondence	:	MONTH/DAY/YEAR *(if letter/memo)*
Type of Claim	:	STATE TYPE OF CLAIM
Alleged Injury	:	STATE INJURY OR INJURIES
Assignment	:	STATE TYPE OF ASSIGNMENT (include number of days assigned to case, evening, daytime, limited surveillance number on hours each day, 4 hours weekend. weekday, 2 man surveillance, surveillance with $ limit, and any other specifics concerning EXACTLY what was requested.

Synopsis

Investigator: Name of Investigator / The Investigative Agency

Date of Investigation: Day of Week / Month / Day / Year; Time
EXAMPLE: Monday, July 7, 2014 (6:00 a.m. - 3:30 p.m.); Tuesday, July 8, 2014 (6:00 a.m. - 3:30 p.m.).

Objectives: Determine Employee's daily activities, degree of disability and employment status. (Be specific. If they want to see how active "on the weekend" say so. State whether it was a rush to see what the employee had planned this day because" he /she cancelled a doctors appointment or therapy visit", etc. If a 2 man investigation state why necessary).

Pertinent Information: *Most Important Category DO NOT JUST SUMMARIZE THE DAY. Dictate the <u>highlights,</u> and special events that specifically portray the employee activity level and physical capability, this is what's important. How does what the employee did relate to his injury and what he is not suppose to be doing? Always indicate how much video documentation was obtained. What significant event or information was developed. Review "assignment sheet" and answer any specific questions the client raised). In most cases it is recommended that he speak to at lease one or two neighbors before* *leaving a surveillance for the day to determine whether there is more information available about your subject that you would not otherwise obtain.*

Then give your recommendation of what needs to be done as a follow-up. Always report this in a separate paragraph so that the reader does not miss it. This is vitally important for us to be able to conduct a complete and thorough investigation. We do not want cases being closed that are not complete.

EXAMPLE
During my day of surveillance .....

1) The employee was very active being first observed at _____ a.m./p.m. as he/she
   (Briefly give a general overview of what the employee did during your surveillance efforts) When describing the Employee's movements, cover the following briefly)
   a. Did the employee exhibit a limp?
   c. Did the employee walk with a cane?
   d. Was the employee observed with any type of orthopedic aid?
   e. Was the employee capable of entering and exiting his vehicle without hesitation or the appearance of stiffness/restriction?
   f. Can the employee drive?
   g. Did the employee partake in any strenuous activity?
   h. Did the employee do any bending, lifting, squatting, sitting or standing for a long period of time.

2) Indicate whether the employee is working? or whether there is any indication that he/she might be?

3) Briefly indicate whether the employee was observed performing, or found involved in any noteworthy activity that may be contradictory to his <u>current allegations</u>.(the specificity concerning movements and physical abilities should be commented on in the actual details. Keep your pertinent information informative, concise and to the point!

In a separate paragraph indicate your efforts to develop NEW or corroborating information about the Employee's activities. What did you determine during you neighborhood contact at the end of the day? This information is necessary to help direct the investigation, utilize time wisely, and focus on obtaining the necessary evidence to defend or verify the claim. **If the employee was found WORKING skip to number 3.**

   a) What did the neighbors have to say regarding the employee's normal everyday activities?

   b) Does what the neighbors say support or contradict your findings?

    c) If the employee is found working...
        1) Proceed to identify co-workers and supervisor.
        2) Verify employment through administration/personnel department.
            a. start date/length of employment
            b. rate of pay/salary
            c. specific job duties/supervisors name

Finally most important, is your thoughts and recommendations on how to proceed. Don't just say I think we need two more days of surveillance. Give your reasons and be specific about what still needs to be done. Review the follow-up suggestions in Chapter 6 or call the office for advise. Any investigator with less than six months of employment should review all verbal reports and follow-up suggestion first with his supervisor before calling a client.

As your last sentence state (Please see page _____ for Details of Investigation).

Physical Description:

1) Race/Color
2) Sex
3) Date of Birth and Age
4) Height
5) Build - Slender/Medium/Muscular/Heavy/Obese
6) Weight
7) Hair Color/Length
8) Facial Hair
9) Eye Color
10) Other Identifying Characteristics

Verbal Report:

1) Date
2) Time
3) How or with who detailed message given? Be specific (voice mail or adjuster/secretary)
4) Full or partial report.
5) Any follow-up instruction by client? If further authorization given was it clearly indicated that additional charges would apply? Was the original limit increased? Is so by what amount? Was a two-man investigation authorized? Is so clearly state so.
6) If **NO** verbal report was requested, state the following:
As requested, no verbal report was made on this file.

BE CAREFUL HOW YOU DOCUMENT ANY DIFFICULTY YOU HAD CONTACTING THE ADJUSTER. WE DO NOT WANT TO OFFEND THE ADJUSTER OR MAKE THEM LOOK BAD TO A SUPERVISOR OR ANYONE ELSE REVIEWING A REPORT.

Do not leave a message asking the adjuster to call the office. Leave a complete message regarding the outcome of your investigation when verbal report is made. Advise that a partial/full report will follow. Advise that you are in the field but if the adjuster should need to reach you they can leave a message at the office for you to call them.

Case Status: Is case open or closed? If the client asked you to diary the case, indicate the diary date when the case is scheduled to do again. Also indicate what may still need to be done once additional authorization is given.

Thank you very much for this opportunity to have been of service. Should you have any questions regarding this investigation, you can contact me at (telephone number of office where you retrieve your messages. Use ONE NUMBER, and NEVER let other Investigator working for you or helping out give different phone numbers. Get use to **branding** and giving out just one number)

Enclosures: List your enclosures. Do not describe in detail, this was done in Documentation caption. Just indicate the number of different pieces of evidence enclosed.

EXAMPLE:

Enclosures: (1) Three still photographs
      (2) One business card
      (3) Copy of occupational license
      (4) Video tape copy (Attorney only)

cc: Joe D. Brown, Esquire
   1289 Tree Limb Lane
   Orlando, Florida 34673

Indicate whether any copy of the report should be forwarded to another party. Instruct your typist to print an extra copy of the report when you are dictating this request. Enclosures should be copies and double prints must be enclosed to send both parties all the indicated enclosures.

If a video tape copy only goes to the attorney make sure this is stated in the enclosure as indicated above.

Details of Investigation

Background Database Internet Research

All surveillance reports are to include this caption regardless of whether a search was conducted. When a search has not been requested, the caption should read "None requested". If there is a search pending, it should then read, "Pending _____ history". (i.e., Criminal, Driver's License, Workers' Compensation, Florida Public Records Search (Nexis Lexis, IRB, TLO, etc...)

When a search has been conducted and the information received address the evidence or enclosures in detail. A few examples are as follows:

Enclosure No. 2 is the FDLE, (State, County) criminal history search requested. This search revealed the subject was most recently found guilty of burglary in June of 2013. According to the arrest information the subject was arrested as he attempted to flee a convenience store at 4:30 am exiting through a broken window in the rear of the store. Unbeknown to the subject the police were on the scene as a silent alarm was triggered some 20 minutes prior to his arrest. Prior to this arrest we also found that in 2009, the subject was prosecuted for Assault, but the charge was subsequently acquitted. The specific details of this case were not available at this time and would have to be ordered from the county archives. Should you require more information of this offense, I would suggest ordering the file, which should take 4-5 days.

The subject's (Employee's) driving history revealed he has had four citations dating back to 2001. The last citation was issued in 2011, for careless driving.

For Workers' Compensation searches report as much information as possible about the claim. Identify the date(s) of the WC claim, lost time, injury, and carrier.

The subject's (Employee's) vehicle history search revealed he currently owns a 2014 Ford Mustang, along with a 2002 Toyota Corolla. The subject's (Employee's) wife (name), is also listed on the registration.

If you have the copy of the search requested (which should always be the case, include the document with the report and refer to it by its enclosure number as indicated above).

After dictating **ANY** DATABASE information always include the following disclaimer: "This information was provided by a third party and should be used as an investigative tool only and should be verified through a separate and independent investigation."

Next go online and check the County Property Appraise to see who owns the house, how much they paid. If the target doesn't own the house secure the landlord/owners name and address in case you need to contact them.

Search all available online county records such as the County Recorder's Office for any civil or criminal filings. Review all available file information on line.

Use your Browser to see what pops up after entering their full name and city.

Any and all information obtained should be listed in your report and captioned prior to initiating the investigation.

A sample of this caption should be as follows:

Internet Search

During a name and address search, I found the claimant and his wife are listed as member of The Villages Dance Club, promoted by Dancers Abound located at 11962 CR101, Suite 101, The Villages, FL 32162. The shop is operated by manager Deb Moss and Jim Shomaker.

On the web the clubs URL is http://danceclub-thevillages.com/index.html. Here I found a picture of the claimant and his wife who are referred to as "George And Martha posing on the dance floor. I found their next event is called the "2014 Dance Off" It will occur in March. Below is a copy of the Clubs Event notice......

EARLY IN YOUR INVESTIGATION YOU MAY ALSO FIND THAT A PRE-SURVEILLANCE INVESTIGATION IS NEEDED TO IDENTIFY THE EMPLOYEE, LOCATE THE RESIDENCE OR DETERMINE A SUITABLE SURVEILLANCE LOCATION. MANY TIMES THIS IS IMPERATIVE ESPECIALLY WHEN A RURAL BOX AND ROUTE NUMBER IS THE ONLY ADDRESS KNOWN.

THE FOLLOWING CAPTIONS ARE **EXAMPLES** OF HOW THIS INFORMATION CAN BE DICTATED.

Pre-Surveillance Investigation - Employee's Residence
<u>Route 5, box 54-A , Ocala Florida 32970</u>   <u>Thursday, February 1, 2014</u>
4:33 p.m.

On the above captioned date, I proceeded to canvass the Anderson Heights area located approximately 16 miles south of S.R. 55 and Hwy. 247 on Samson Rd. also known as Route 6. The Employee's residence was found to be located in the Samson Mobile Home Park on lot A. Specifically, the Employee's residence is a doublewide mobile home, which is yellow in color with white trim and is in excellent condition. Underneath the carport, which is just to the left of the residence I observed no vehicles.

Immediately after my arrival in the area I observed an elderly female subject, who is apparently the Employee's wife, arrive at the residence on a bicycle. After placing the bicycle underneath the carport, the female subject then entered the residence where her activities were no longer observable.

At this point, having located the residence and familiarizing myself with the area, I elected to depart the area and return on the following day.

Pre-Surveillance Investigation-Employee's Residence
2115 Nottingham Rd., Melbourne, Florida 32935   Thursday, February 1, 2014
4:30p.m.

During the late afternoon hours of the above captioned date, I was in the general area of the Employee's residence on an unrelated matter and elected to make a personal visit to his residence for the purpose of making some general observations as well as familiarizing myself with the area. Upon my arrival in the area, I found that the Employee's residence is located in a middle, working class, residential area with in the city limits of Melbourne, Florida.

Specifically, the Employee's residence is a one story, single family home that is light brown in color with brown trim. I noted that the residence was in very good condition and the lawn was immaculately landscaped. Parked on the swell of the road, directly in front of the Employee's residence was a silver Mazda pickup truck, which was attached to a small utility trailer, bearing Florida registration AI5-62T. I noted the trailer contained various types of lawn maintenance equipment. The side of the trailer stated "Timely Lawn Service".

Also, at the time of my arrival, I was fortunate enough to have the opportunity to directly observe the employee. The employee, who was standing underneath the carport, which is on the southeast side of the residence is a white male, approximately 49 years of age, approximately 6'1" tall, weighs 195 pounds and has brown hair, which is graying. I noted the employee was wearing a T-shirt, blue jeans, and black rubber soled shoes. I observed the employee drinking a mug of coffee while looking about the neighborhood. After just a few moments, the employee turned and entered his residence at which point his activities were no longer observable. Not wanting to arouse suspicion, I elected to depart the area.

WHEN NO PRE-SURVEILLANCE IS NECESSARY THE INVESTIGATION WILL PROCEED ONTO THE ACTUAL SURVEILLANCE.

Surveillance - Employee's Residence
1276 Deer Lake Circle Apopka Florida 32712   Monday, July 7, 2014
6:00 p.m.

The first day of a surveillance is typically started at 6:00 a.m. during the week. Make certain you leave early enough to account for your travel time. Our first objective is to determine whether the subject may be gainfully employed. Once this is determined we then will concentrate on the severity of the injury. What can and can't the employee do? The more activity we observe and document, the better prepared we will be in defending the claim against exaggeration or outright fraud.

01) State full residential address in the caption.
02) Briefly provide driving directions to the residence. If the address is in a metropolitan area just provide directions from the nearest WELL-KNOWN intersection. If the address is a rural area then give more explicit directions.
03) Indicate telephone number and whether published or unpublished.
04) List persons residing with the employee whenever possible (since dictation will occur after the investigation, this information should be known).
05) Describe type of residence (single family/multifamily/condominium/townhouse/apartment).
06) Color and other identifying characteristics
07) Economic status of neighborhood (lower, middle or upper working class)
08) Social Environment (adult community/retirement community; closely knit residential community/rural sparsely populated community)
09) Maintenance (Well maintained/in need of repair/manicured lawn/trash & debris everywhere)
10) Upon arrival were there any lights on in or outside of the residence?
11) Were there any signs that some early morning movement may have already taken place?
12) Identify all vehicles at the residence fully color/make/model/tag numbers. (later you will run the tag and put more information in the report under the caption "Dept. Of Highway Safety and Motor Vehicles"
12) Indicate the position of the vehicles in relationship to the residence.
13) Do any of the vehicles exhibit a registration sticker correlating to the Employee's month of birth?
15) Report any other observations noted.
16) Describe and assume your surveillance position.
EXAMPLE: I assumed a surveillance position approximately 200 yards north of the Employee's property. This position afforded me an unobstructed view of both the Employee's front door and vehicle parked in the driveway.

Always start each step you take with a caption. Your report should flow like a detailed story. Take your time to ensure that your complete thoughts and observations are expressed.

As you dictate your report, remember your focus, concentration should be on the employee and his/her movements. Don't go into detail about the description of neighbors, the milkman or other less pertinent observations. No weather forecasts please (we need to do surveillance in the rain because we can not guarantee the weather. Furthermore many people go to work in the rain! Employment is our primary concern. Case management is also important and if you try to work on only sunny days, you will fall behind quickly with your caseload.)

Details regarding the Employee's identify, conduct, movements, affiliations, associations, transactions, reputation or character are your focal points. Your observations, investigative findings concerning these involvement's need to be documented and well detailed in your report. Dictate in complete sentences and allow the reader to follow your line of thinking.

During your surveillances you will routinely run the registration of the vehicle(s) observed at the residence to determine which one the subject may own or operate. You will also "run" the tag registrations of the people stopping by to visit the employee.

Initially your first call will usually occur around 8:00 - 9:00 a.m. The closest tag agency and telephone number to call can be found in the company handbook and will depend on the area you are working in. Once you make the call you should be aware of all the information available. The following caption is an example of how this information should be captioned. The information listed below the caption should be obtained and incorporated into the dictated paragraph under this caption.

EXAMPLE

Department of Highway Safety & Motor Vehicles
Vehicle Registration Information   Monday, July 7, 2014
8:33 a.m.

Identify make, model and year of vehicle
Subject's full name
Date of Birth
Address that appears on registration
Driver's License number
Lien holder
Anything unusual or contradictory to the information already known

SAMPLE DICTATION

I contacted the above agency to determine the owner of the late model pearl colored Dodge Caravan bearing the Florida registration of 5AB-CDI parked in the driveway. This vehicle was identified as a 1992 Dodge Caravan registered to a Jim F. Brown whose address was listed as 1276 Deer Lake Circle Apopka, Florida 32712. Jim Brown's date of birth was indicated as July 7, 1950 and his driver's license number was B420-678-50-287. Furthermore, the lien holder on this vehicle was identified as Marty's Buy Here Pay Here located at 560 Semoran Blvd., Altamonte, Florida.

10:30 a.m.

By 10:30 a.m., you are requested to determine whether the employee is inside the residence. This is done solely to insure that we are not sitting on an empty house or the Employee's prior residence before he moved to Europe. This is NOT a time to pretext the EMPLOYEE or ANY family member for information. Therefore, information concerning ONLY whether or not the employee is at home needs to be addressed. DO NOT go into any details concerning your contact.

If you are required to leave your surveillance position to make the above telephone call, indicate the time you left the area.

EXAMPLE

10:28 a.m.

Finding no early morning movement by the employee, I elected to momentarily depart my surveillance position to proceed and verify the Employee's presence in the residence.

10:30 a.m.

Although the employee had not been seen, I confirmed that he/she was, in fact, inside the residence. (To determine how to make these discreet findings refer to using pretexts)

10:37 a.m.

Having confirmed that the employee was in fact inside the residence, I returned to the Employee's neighborhood to resume my investigation. Upon my return, I noticed no movement by either vehicle at the residence nor any sign of the employee or any other subject outside. In anticipation of any possible activity, I immediately resumed my surveillance position.

EXAMPLE

10:30 a.m.

As suspected, it was determined that no one appeared to be inside the residence. Apparently either the employee had spent the preceding night away from the residence or he had left prior to my early morning arrival (In this case you would proceed with a thorough neighborhood inquiry to determine why the employee was not home). This would be done BEFORE you leave the area for the day.

Sometimes you need to advise the reader that you are moving onto another step so, follow me. This can be done by first prefacing your move before actually doing it.

Example: It was apparent that the telephone number provided by the employee was not for this Deer Lake Dr. address. I, therefore, elected to contact a Nationwide Database to ascertain what address did correlate to this number.

National Database -Telephone Number Records Search
(407) 933-2010

Through this Database I determined that the telephone number listed was actually for the business, Claims Resource, Incorporated. The account address was identified as 414 Greenbrier Ave, Suite 62, Celebration, Florida 34747.

I proceeded to contact this business in order to determine what if any association exists between the employee and this business.

Telephone Contact - The Business
(407) 933-2010   Monday, July 7, 2014
11:30 a.m.

In the example above, I continued to move the reader from one step of my investigation into the next.

During this conversation let's assume the telephone call developed an address for the employee. Once obtaining this information we then proceeded to the address to verify that the employee did in fact reside at this location.

Employee's Residence-333 Kiwi Court - Casselberry, Florida 32707
12:15 p.m. VT

Once at this location I immediately spotted the employee out side cutting the grass pushing a conventional lawn mower. I immediately began shooting video of this activity. From the on-set it was apparent that the mower was an older model and not self propelled. The employee, who was leaning forward at approximately a 45 degree angle was sweating profusely as it appeared the lawn was severely over grown etc……

(Make note of the **VT** in this caption which denotes Video was taken. Be certain that the time on the tape and the times in your report MATCH. If the times are off for some reason it must be addressed whenever the video is mentioned).

Verbal Report
3:40 p.m.

Subsequent to your surveillance efforts a report to the client needs to be made. This will be your opportunity to bring the client up to date and also advise him/her of your recommended follow-up. Verbal reports are most often given at the end of your authorized investigation.

I HAVE LISTED SOME HELPFUL HINTS THAT MAY MAKE YOUR DICTATION GO A BIT SMOOTHER.

Quite often we say things in our reports that although occurred exactly as we dictated, can mislead the client into thinking that we were not as thorough as we should have been and, therefore, a margin for error appears to exist.

For example, let's say your report goes as follows:

> A white female approximately 5' tall, 140 pounds, blonde hair and appearing to be approximately 42 years of age exited the residence. This subject resembled the description provided by your office, and thus, for the remainder of this report will be referred to as the employee.

In actuality, having read this report, it seems that you immediately assumed that this subject was the employee merely from the fact that she resembled the characteristics of the employee. In a true sense, this is usually how we first identify a subject and then later proceed in verifying that it is, in fact, the employee. Therefore, at no time while you're writing the report several days later, should there be any doubt in your mind whether or not this subject was or was not the employee.

Therefore, this sentence should start out simply as;

> The employee, a white female approximately 5' tall, 140 pounds, blonde hair and appearing to be approximately 42 years of age exited the residence.

This eliminates any doubt that may be placed in our client's mind that the subject we followed was not, in fact, the employee and only assumed to be based on her description.

Later in your report you can also provide other information based on the vehicle's registration and perhaps a discreet conversation with the subject, which further corroborated your identification of the employee.

Surveillance **LOST EMPLOYEE**

It's not difficult to lose a employee during a "tail" as we have all found out. Taking the time to word this misfortune may help ease the reader into what you are about to say. Once I read a report where the investigator had followed the employee all over town then merely stated that he lost the employee at a red light.

Many times intervening traffic, construction and traffic lights are the true demons in this business. Take the time to explain the circumstances that prohibited your continuing efforts. Don't go into detail three pages long but give a simple explanation. Always explain that you continued in the same general area as the employee was last seen and thoroughly canvassed the area in an attempt to relocate the employee. I also think it sounds a little bit better if we refer to our relationship with the employee as "contact".

Example: I lost contact with the employee due to intervening traffic at the intersection of A1A and Boogie Board Rd. I continued south on A1A for several miles, thoroughly canvassing the area, however, I found no opportunity to relocate the employee.

And finally, always remember to **RETURN** to the Employee's residence in case he was only running an errand. Many times you will find that the employee returns to his residence within a short time period. He may also be carrying evidence to provide a clue as to where he was. It's typical to lose someone and observe him return home 45 minutes later with a large bag possibly bearing the green and orange K-Mart insignia on the side. It's doesn't take a Ph.D. to surmise where he was. Make note of this observation and then continue with your surveillance efforts. Then stay an hour or two longer into the day to make up for the time the employee was out of your view. If you have nothing else scheduled for this day, it is recommended you get a good surveillance position and remain in the area UNTIL the employee returns home. This way we will at least get good film of them returning to the residence and who knows what they might unload from the vehicle or do immediately following their return. Chances are this may put off an urgent need to work the case again the following day.

Surveillance **PHOTOS/VIDEO**

Photographic documentation in every report should be an objective of any company reporting requirements. It's easy to tell the investigators who have learned the video capture technique and have it down to a simple and easy process however for those less skilled with PC's it may be a challenge they need to spend more time on to over come. With the ability to make prints from your Video, you should avoid stopping video to shoot from a still digital camera. Digital cameras are really obsolete unless you need very high quality photographs and are not doing  surveillance. In this case the save digital file will be all you need to save and send your client. The digital file can also be inserted into your report.

In order to extract a photograph from a digital video recording you will need a Video Capturing device and software from companies like Dazzle and Pinnacle. These devices are made up of a hardware device in which a cable runs from the device to your computer by a USB cord. The device itself will hook up with your digital camera through an S Cable, RCA Composite Cables or DV Cable.

Remember in order to capture a photo with the time and date stamp called meta data, a video capture device MUST be used. The same holds true for the actual video. You can not simply drag and drop video from your camera to a computer file and still get the time and date stamp (or at least not without some very high tech video programs).

Surveillance **P.O. Box**

Whenever only a post office box address is given, we must dictate the procedures we initiated to obtain an actual physical address. If perhaps a previous report provided directions to the Employee's residence then report this as well. Never merely start a surveillance under the caption of a post office box address because, it's obvious that the employee doesn't live in a mailbox. Whichever is the case, it needs to be clearly indicated in the report.

REMEMBER

The examples are not meant to be complete and comprehensive for all circumstances. Each set of circumstances will demand different actions and reporting. First and foremost be persistent and use your imagination at all times.

Chapter Eleven
Common Investigations & Reports

I. Cheating Spouse
II. Child Custody
III. Child Support
IV. Slip and Fall
V. Wrongful Death
VI. SIU/Insurance Claims Investigations
VII. Domestic / Infidelity
VIII. Computer Forensic

11. Examples of Common Investigations & Reports

In this section I have put together a reference guide with several different types of investigations I worked so you can see my procedures, style, wording and format.

Cheating Spouse

Many newcomers to the industry will find themselves working Divorce Cases, Cheating Spouses and Cheating Significant Others. This is an excellent area to begin your career as the clients will be less sophisticated and more likely to assist you. I worked a case where the woman had devoted 20 plus years to her husband who was busy building a successful business with of course the assistance of his wife. But the husband took an interest in the 20 year old office's marketing girl and soon went astray or at least that's what my client felt. She needed surveillance on her husband to see if he was cheating. The husband never gave any indication that he was intimate with the young girl. He insisted that his wife was just being jealous and imagining things. The cheating spouse thought he was too sharp to be caught. He had blacked out windows on his Cadillac and the two would make rendezvous secretly in a busy hospital parking lot. He would even take her to his Cocoa Beach Condominium where he would drive into the building secured under ground parking and take up to unit via an indoor elevator all outside the scope of any tailing investigator.

Child Custody Case

You may find yourself investigating a parent for a Child Custody Case and may be following the subject to show he has personal issues such as drinks excessively, uses drugs or has a lifestyle not otherwise conducive to raising or having minors in his/her custody. In a case I recently worked, the woman stated her husband was basically a functioning alcoholic however she realized that his constant intoxication was putting her children at risk and she wanted supervised visitation. To prove a point she wanted me to pick him up after work and document (through video) his activities. After work he went directly to a local bar for happy hour. I proceeded inside and observed him drink four beers in one hour. I recorded video of him drinking and secured the name of the bartender and the date and time of our visit so that a receipt could be obtained documenting the subject's purchases. After the happy hour he drove to a convenience store to pump gas and bought a beer. I was fortunate enough to get video of him opening the tab and drinking it while still in the gas stations parking lot. He then proceeded across town and stopped at his favorite hangout to play darts and shoot pool. Inside, I observed him drink four more beers and do two shots over a three hour period of time. At 11:30 p.m. he headed outside and got in his car to drive home. The video was used to prove a point that her husband was not capable of restraining his drinking. In fact her husband had two previous DUI's and currently did not have a valid license.

Child Support Case

The subject claimed he was injured and did not have any income to meet his support obligations and wanted the child support reduced. The client knew he was working and stated that his new girlfriend just wanted all the money and was not concerned with the wellbeing of his children from the previous marriage. The client needed to show the judge that her husband was working and that the support should continue and in no way be reduced. (See sample report following page)

Sample Child Support Dispute

CONFIDENTIAL

September 29, 2013

Gary Shady, Esquire	Re:	Your File No.	: Dibson Vs Smith
LAW OFFICES		Addt'l File No.	: N/S
1750 N. Montgomery Ave.		Our File No.	: FL-0410-DOM
Maitland, FL 32751		Subject	: Andrew Smith
		SSN	: N/S
		D/L	: N/S

Assignment Received : March 2010
Previous Correspondence : None
Type of Claim : Domestic
Assignment : Determine the work activities of Mr. Andrew Smith who resides at 8244 Stark Lane Circle, Maitland, Florida 32751. Mr. Smith reports not working and may have a suspended Driver's License and is not supposed to be driving.

Synopsis

Investigator: John Bilyk/ www.claimsresource.cc / 877-274-2000

Dates of Investigation: Monday, April 5, 2010 and Spot Check Thursday, September 23, 2010.

Pertinent Information: I proceeded with surveillance in order to determine if the subject was working.

Surveillance Subject's Residence -8211 Stark Lane Circle,
Maitland, Florida 32751   Monday, April 5, 2010
5:24 a.m.

Due to the subject's history of working within the construction field, I arrived in the early morning hours to document his activities. At the above time, I noticed no cars or trucks parked in the driveway leading to the attached single car garage. There however is also common parking or extra spaces across for the townhouse units. Located here I observed a maroon Ford King Ranch Pick-up which had been described as the subject's primary vehicle. To the left of this vehicle was a white SUV and to the right of that was a large white cargo van. I observed no detectable lights on inside the residence nor any indication of early morning movement.

7:22 a.m. VT

A blond haired female appearing to be in her 40's exited the townhouse through the privacy fence gate leading to the parking area. She entered the white SUV and departed the area.

7:39 a.m.- 7:41 a.m. VT

The subject exited the Townhouse's fenced in entrance and proceeded to walk to the white cargo van parked next to the Ford King Ranch truck. He opened the rear of the cargo van apparently checking the contents inside. He was dressed in blue jeans and a blue t-shirt.

7:50 a.m. VT

The male subject exited again this time with a large dog which he proceeded to walk in the grassy area in front of the parked vehicles. The subject was now wearing a baseball cap and was smoking a cigarette. He then returned to the townhouse.

7:54 a.m. VT

The subject exited again, went to the Ford truck then walked back towards the house then was seen again entering the driver's side door of the white van. The subject then proceeded to drive the vehicle heading in a southeasterly direction, south on Orange Ave., left on Solana, left on Webster, right on Pennsylvania which turned into Lake Sue, right on Winter Park Drive, left on Corrine and right on Osprey Ave.

8:20 a.m.-8:28 a.m. VT

The subject stopped at 3722 Ibis Drive, Orlando. I was advised that the subject reportedly had his driving privileges revoked however he was driving this white van bearing the Florida registration X76-8BB. As he arrived he remained seated in his van as another individual who had been waiting for him walked to the driver's door and engaged

in conversation. This subject has a long brown hair he wears in a pony tail. He was wearing a baseball cap as well and a tan shirt with advertisement on the back. He was also driving a tan colored pick-up truck. Our subject appeared to be going over things with him and then the pony tailed male departed.

8:43 a.m. – 8:59 a.m. VT

After conversing with the male in the tan truck, our subject parked his van and walked over to another large male appearing to be around 6'4" tall and weighing around 300 pounds working on the exterior of a private residence. He had a white pick-up truck parked around the other side of the property. His tag was obscured, but it was a Lake County Tag. Our subject then walked around with a large coffee cup in his hand, went inside and spoke to the owner and was observed several times traversing the property and meeting with the large male worker present putting using an impact hammer drill to remove the fake or faux exterior brick from the block house. Our subject was apparently there over seeing this males work. I would later learn that they are removing all the fake brick and then resurfacing the house with stucco.

9:02 a.m.

After spending about 15 minutes at this house our subject then left the large worker behind and re-entered the cargo van's driver's seat and again drove himself out of the area. Traveling right on Glenridge, left on Lakemont Ave., right on Mizell Ave., right on Perth Lane, right on Greene drive and left on Brookshire Avenue.

9:16 a.m. –9:22 a.m. VT

The subject arrived at another private residence this one located at 5230 Fitzwalter Drive. Here the subject first went inside for several minutes then came back outside to remove some tool bags which he then carried inside.

At this point, it appeared the subject was running at least a crew of two. I was unsure if he was working for himself or another company. It was apparent he was working, and while he was in Winter Park, I proceeded back over to the first house.

Private Residence -3722 Ibis Drive, Orlando

I parked my vehicle out of sight of the property and walked up to the large male working by himself removing the fake brick on the house. He had removed nearly all of the brick on the carport side of the house. I advised I had a similar home with the same fake brick and wanted to know what it would cost to remove it. I asked him for his companies name and he stated that he worked for a guy called "blue". I could tell though that he was thinking about perhaps getting my job for himself. I asked for "blue's" number and he gave me his. He said he was Craig and I could reach him at 352.321.5855.

I next proceeded back to 5230 Fitzwalter Drive and as I arrived the owner, a young dark haired female, was just backing out of her driveway in a red compact. Seeing that our subject was now gone, I rolled down my window and stated was there a worker here earlier? Her eyes opened wide like I had just stolen her most precious secret and she said no? I said he told me to meet him here and that he was just at the residence. But she maintained that look and insisted no one was at the residence. At this point, either she was lying or she wasn't awake or home when he got there and already left. But the red car was there when he arrived and she was leaving in the same red car. I am not quite certain about this situation, but the video shows he went into the residence at 5230 Fitzwalter Drive.

Telephone Contact Ms. Lynn Dibson 407.461.6677

I relayed the above details to Ms. Dibson and asked if Andrew goes by the name of "blue" and she said yes, that his nickname. I then told her about the pony tailed male and she said he has been a worker for her ex-husband for some time. I advised that it appeared possible the home on Ibis may have had a new gravel roof and perhaps Mr. Smith is getting leads from his current girlfriend's families roofing business, but I had not confirmed anything about how he is getting his work.

Orange County Property Appraiser

As a cursory effort, I searched the records for the owners of 3722 Ibis Drive, Orlando and found them to be Layton and Lisa Marie Slev. I checked 411 for a phone listing, but found no listings for a Lee at that address. At some point, we may want to contact them to learn how they heard about our subject if by word of month, another

job/homeowner, referral from the roofing company or an advertisement some where.

At this point, having identified two jobs with just one days or 5 hours effort, it appears that our subject is very much in business and also driving.

<u>Continued Spot Check</u>   Thursday, September 23, 2010

I returned to the area and noticed the Mr. Smith now has ladder racks and tow ladders on top of the white van. It appears he has been accumulating tools for his job and further fitting the van to support more tools. I took a photograph while in the area. You can see the comparison pictures between what the van looked like in April to what it looks like in September.

Case Status: Closed

Thank you for the opportunity to be of service.

Should you have any questions regarding this investigation, please contact my office by phone or via the internet at cases@claimsresource.cc

****End of Report****

Slip and Fall

I routinely investigate slip and fall accidents and during the course of these investigations, I look for any deficiencies in the floor or interview witnesses to rule out any debris left on the floor. I go so far as to determine the amount of cashier register receipts so I can determine the number of patrons visiting that store a day. I interview the manager and determine the store floor is monitored every 15 minutes. I have even taken statements of people coming and going from the store asking them have they ever felt the store was un-kept or the floors slippery. I take this information along with the statistics that 500 patrons visit the store on a daily basis and that this is the only fall that has ever occurred in the ketchup isle to create doubt about what happened. With no noted debris, a history of no prior accidents and witnesses feeling the floors are safe and not slippery was this really a slip and fall or was this a trip or staged fall. We have all tripped or slipped at one time. What makes this a libel incident is when negligence enters into the situation. But if a person comes into a store and is not paying attention and trips on their own feet, the business owner did nothing wrong.

In my 30 years in the business I have found that there is no shortage of professional con artists out there faking slip and falls. One that comes to mind occurred in south Florida in around 2010. I was given a clam made by a woman who fell in a large beauty supply chain. It turns out that the woman went to the hospital and had a $500 CAT scan done on her head she stated she hit on the floor. The whole bill was around $1200.00. The woman very politely called the insurance company and said just reimburse me the $1200.00. The adjuster ran a claims history report on the woman and found over 15 claims for similar activities. Either this woman was the unluckiest person in the world or she was a professional claimant. What was more interesting was that she had another incident the same day at a large pet supermarket, only a block away from the beauty products chain. I went to the pet supermarket and spoke to the manager who out m in touch with his risk management department. I learned the same woman had allegedly slipped and fell, hit her head and went to the hospital. The bill was #1200.00. In fact the bill submitted to them was the same bill submitted to my client. The scam here is to go to the hospital have some medical attention they send the bill to multiple locations. The other scam is that she never intended to pay the hospital either. During my investigation, I found the address she used was a mail box center. The center had two forms of ID a student ID and a business ID. Both were completely fraudulent. I called the woman several times attending try to get her to meet with me so I could determine her true identity. I even wanted to stake out the mail box location, but she hadn't paid the bill for two months and apparently only used the address to imitate the claim. The mail center was locking her box and the scam artist knew at this point going to that box was not a good idea. This was an experienced professional claimant who just happened to pick the wrong insurance company this time.

Unfortunately not all companies have access to the ISO claim reporting system. So those without the resources to check a claimant's prior claim history will continue to support the efforts of these scam artists.

Wrongful Death Suit

I was asked to investigate a suit for wrongful death filed by the decedent's mother. She claimed a wrongful death suit and "damages" for the loss of her son whom she loved dearly. She stated that her son had been rear ended in an auto accident and severely hurt. She stated that he was on pain medication which he did not like to take. She further stated that he was unable to work due to his injury and subsequently became depressed then shot himself all as a result of the car accident.

Well going into this case, I knew I had investigated hundreds of auto accident and injured claimants that had not shot themselves. There had to be more to this case and the adjuster told me that it was suggested that the claimant may have been Baker Acted in the past meaning that someone thought he was a harm to himself and he was admitted and retained for some type of psychiatric evaluation.

I immediately thought to myself, that this guy had some underlying psychiatric issues I had to document. With his address being in Tallahassee, I also thought maybe he was a student. I wanted to determine if perhaps while at college he was known as a heavy partier or drug user. What I found was a history of mental health issues including Chronic Panic Attack and that if left untreated had a documented high rate of suicides. (See sample report following page)

Sample Wrongful Death Suit

C O N F I D E N T I A L

August 26, 2009

Mr. Steve Johnson	Re:	Your File No.	:	UHV8646
TRAVELERS		Addtl File No.	:	N/S
7840 Woodland Center		Our File No.	:	FL-0809-006
Tampa, FL 33614		Insured	:	CLABE & KERRY POLK
		Subject	:	Thomas Frashline
		SSN	:	589-32-9442
		D/L	:	5/29/2008

Assignment Received	:	August 4, 2009
Previous Correspondence	:	None
Type of Claim	:	Auto
Assignment	:	Identify potential witnesses and sources of information pertinent to the investigation. Secure information concerning the reported Baker Acting of the Claimant. Identify information concerning the claimant's past, background and relationship with his mother.

Synopsis

Investigator: John Bilyk/www.claimsresource.cc / 877/274-2000

Date of Investigation: Wednesday, August 5, 2009; Tuesday, August 18, 2009; Thursday, August 19, 2009; Friday, August 20, 2009; Monday, August 24, 2009 and Tuesday, August 25, 2009.

Pertinent Information: On Wednesday, August 5, 2009, I proceeded to the claimant's former address where he lived in off campus housing near the University of Tallahassee. The claimant's building is located in a heavily wooded townhouse community about one mile from campus. The townhouses are occupied by mostly college students and most are privately owned. The claimant's unit is exactly the same as the others in the complex and is a three unit townhouse building with units marked A,B &C. The deceased claimant reportedly occupied the center unit "B". I found Ms. Annie Greco living to the right in unit C and unit A was empty and for rent by Spirit Reality with a telephone number of 850.877.4343. All of the occupants now living in Unit B are new move-ins. I spoke to Ms. Greco whose Dad purchased her unit two years ago. She was aware of the deceased claimant, but never knew him personally and never spoke to him. She stated the house was pretty quiet and she never had any interaction with any of the occupants.

I next expanded my search and found another resident in one building over located to the right in unit 1348-A. This subject Arty Gallegos is a senior at FSU and also lived within 20 feet of the claimant's unit. The two other units 1348-A and B were further away but had occupants that were new to the area.

I expanded my search to the left of the claimant's unit to 1352-B. This subject Amanda Russo is a graduate student and has lived in her unit for 4 years. Her unit is about 30 feet away. She also did not know the claimant nor had she had any interaction with him. She too lived there through the summer of 2008 and stated the residence was pretty quiet and not known as a party house or partying residents.

Background Check - Leon County Civil Records Search Tallahassee, FL

I next proceeded to check County records for any notation regarding the deceased. I searched records from 9/30/1953 to the present 8/5/2009 and found no entries involving our subject.

I did find that the claimant's townhouse was owned by Aaron and Scott Brummett. They apparently purchased the property on March 5, 2008, from Earl and Amanda Simpson. The purchase price was $130,000 and the transaction was recorded in the official Leon County Clerks Office and can be found in Book 3822 Page 1912. The Brummetts therefore would have been the landlords for the deceased.

Criminal Background Check - Leon County Sheriff's Office Tallahassee, FL

I also checked local criminal records and again found no entry for the subject based on his name, SSN and DOB.

Criminal Background - Pinellas County Sheriff's Office, Clearwater, Florida

Here I identified one record for Thomas Michael Frashline, Case # CTC0002447NCPIN. This case involved our subject being charged on August 30, 2000 for Smoking in School.

Pinellas County Civil Records Search

Once again I found no civil records involving the claimant and no notation of a Baker Act.

Criminal Background - Hillsboro County, Tampa, FL

Again I searched the computer criminal county records under the subject's name but found no entry.

Hillsboro County Civil Records Search

Again I found no civil record and no notation of the claimant being Baker Acted.

Locate Witnesses

I next turned my attention to locating the possible witnesses initially identified only as the claimant's mother and ex-girlfriend. Through a background database I identified the claimant's mother as Ms. Mary Ann Frashline, residing at 40 Pelican Place, Palm Harbor, FL.

I next identified the ex-girlfriend as Amber Angelo. Through database searches and address cross reference, I found an address shared by both the deceased and Ms. Angelo. This address was 12239 Country White Circle, Tampa, FL 33635-6279.

Telephone Update

As requested I spoke to the Claims Handler, Mr. Johnson and learned that we can not contact the claimant's mother, but to go ahead and proceed with a neighborhood investigation in Palm Harbor. He also stated that he had more statements from other witnesses on CD and he would forward them to me.

On Monday, August 10, 2009, I received the CDs for the statements of Mary Ann Frashline, Paul Casamiro, Nicholas De George, Jeremy Borders and Eric Vanderlaan. I listened to these recordings but found they contained no personal identifying information on the witnesses. I re-contacted Mr. Johnson who indicated he has requested contact information for the subjects but has not heard back from the Claimant's Attorney. Therefore aside from Ms. Anthony, and the claimant's mother, I had no current address for Mr. Casamiro, De George or Border.

Background Database Searches
Locate Witnesses Tuesday, August 18, 2009

I initiated preliminary efforts to locate the most current addresses for the witnesses and ran background Database searches on each subject. I received the following addresses for each subject:

Jeremy Brantlyn Borderes- SSN 259-67-xxxx DOB 3/23/1987
July 2009 – address 1851 Perimeter Road, Fernandina Beach, FL 32034-1952

Paulo Alexander Casamiros- SSN 037-58-xxx DOB 11/6/1985
135 Dixie Drive, Tallahassee, FL 32304-3018

Eric Robert Vanderlander- SSN 592-64-xxxx DOB 10/19/1984
135 Dixie Drive, Tallahassee, FL 32304-3018
Telephone # 850-597-9179

Nicholas Georges- SSN 493-02-xxxx- DOB 8/5/1984
July 2009- 13738 Bluewater Circle, Orlando, FL 32828-8317
Telephone Number 727-600-6649

Once having addresses identified, I proceeded to contact the witnesses. I first made a personal visit to Ms. Anthony's residence.

Recorded Witness Statement
Ms. Allendina Amber Angelo
DOB 2/5/1986 / SSN 593-32-xxxx / Cellular 727.899.1223
1239 Country White Circle,
Tampa, FL 33635-6279   Thursday, August 20, 2009

I made contact with Ms. Anthony in the evening at her house in west, Tampa. Here she resides wither current Fiancé' Mark Sebben. I discussed my visit at great length with both the witness and her Fiancé before being invited inside to start the recorded statement.

During the statement, the witness stated that she knew the claimant, (Thomas Frashline) for about three years and lived with him for over a year from 2007 – 2008. She stated that when she first met him he stated <u>she saved his life for another year and told her he was throwing a gun he owned in a lake near his house.</u> Apparently, this was not the first time he referenced a gun either. She stated he told her he was arrested for selling a firearm in school or to a school mate. She stated the claimant never finished school or graduated and attended Palm Harbor University High School. According to the witness Thomas stated he experimented with Acid and knew he heavily used Marijuana. He also told her he was involved in a lot of school fighting. She did not know him in H.S. and actually went to another school. She stated that ever since she knew him he smoked a lot of Marijuana. In fact, during the time she knew him he held one job working at Target but lost the job because of panic attacks and throwing up on the job. Prior to his job at Target he sold Marijuana for a living. She stated that he could not function without constant Marijuana use. He smoked to go to Grocery shopping, he smoked to go to Wal-Mart, he even smoked just to play video games. She stated he was the type of person that had a mind that just would not stop and Marijuana seemed to calm him down. He was definitely a handful though and she thought she could change him but found it was just not possible. She stated he was severely depressed probably Bi-Polar and needed medical attention. This was out of the question though because Thomas never liked to take any type of prescription medication. She confirmed that he did not speak to his Mother, Sister or older Brother, nor did they have any thing to do with him. She stated she would be the one that tried to force the family to get together. She stated she made Thomas go to mostly birthday parties where they met at a local restaurant. They did not get together for Christmas or Thanksgiving. She stated that she told the claimant she was ending their relationship around the end of January beginning of February 2008, after the Bucs playoff game and that evening he threatened to kill himself by trying to walk into traffic. This occurred at the intersection of Tampa Road and US19. This was the night that another friend (Jarred) called the Police and the claimant was Baker Acted for around three days. According to Ms. Anthony, the claimant's mother got him out even though she begged her to let him stay there. And once he was out, he came back to Ms. Anthony's home to live and slept on the couch. She wanted the claimant to leave he was depressing, didn't want to work and was costing her money. She was in college taking night classes and working during the day. She was emotionally tired, financially indebt and he was no help. He would have his panic attacks in the middle of the night wake up to walk around the block or throw up. He was a mess and while she initially thought she could help him, she realized she couldn't. She truly cared for him but the toll was too great and she didn't get any help from Thomas, mother. She originally spoke to his mother about him coming back to live with her, but when she tried to call Ms. Frashline she would not answer. The claimant also tried to call her but she did not respond. The witness wanted him gone and found a mutual friend Nicholas Georges in Tallahassee who was going to school there and had an extra room. So the witness drove the now deceased claimant, to Tallahassee and dropped him off. The witness also stated that Thomas told her he lost his job in Tallahassee because of Panic Attacks. The witness told me another person I should contact was Bill Hoyland (727.612.7532. He was apparently present the night the claimant wanted to kill himself after the break-up by walking into traffic.

<u>Bill Hoyland-727.612.7532</u>

I found this number was a pay as you go number and it was currently out of minutes. The witness, Ms. Angelo told me this may happen and to keep trying it.

Neighborhood Investigation – 40 Pelican Place,
Palm Harbor, FL 31790   Friday, August 21, 2009

Here I canvassed the area and spoke to all the neighbors on both side of the claimant's former address. I also determined and spoke to Mr. Foss who bought Ms. Mary Ann Frashline's house nearly 1.5 years ago. In fact, I learned that she moved prior to the claimant's suicide. Mr. Foss did not know anything about the family other than possibly they were having financial problems and needed to sell the house. The Frashline house is located at the end of a dead end cul-de-sac. I contacted all of the residents within close proximity to the residence.

50 Pelican Place

These tenants have two small children and while they knew of the claimant they only saw him occasionally outside. The father, Jerry-stated that he recalls the claimant on the phone outside and remembers he had long hair and looked ruff. He stated he would sometime make his presence known to the claimant because he sometimes would speak loudly on the phone using obscenities or sounding angry. Aside from these brief interactions, he also recalled the neighbor on the other side of the claimant's house, identified as Merilyn Yount telling him Ms. Mary Ann Frashline "has gone through a lot with that boy"

30 Pelican Place

This residence is owned by The Yount's, but they now rent the home and the renters were no at home at the time. I left a note asking them to have their landlord contact me at her convenience.

60 Pelican Place- 727.424.4316

This address is occupied by the McClish's. They had no information to offer and did not have any interaction with the family.

20 Pelican Place

This is an older couple and while they recall a fight at the residence, they did not know which boys were which only that when he went to try top break it up someone said "old man get out of here". Obviously there was a lack of respect for the man which represented to his wife a dangerous situation and she pleaded for his to come back which he did. The woman stated she recalled the police coming to the area afterwards.

Ms. Dorothy Mraz

Ms. Mraz has lived on the corner for the past 20 years and knew Ms. Frashline and her family. She knew the two boys, the claimant and his older brother but did not have much to say about them. She stated they came and went from the area and she really did not know anything about their personal life. She too offered that the closest neighbor to the Frashlines was Ms. Merlynn Yount, but she has moved out of the neighborhood, but was believed to still live somewhere in Palm Harbor. Ms. Mraz stated that Ms. Frashline babysat Ms. Yount's children occasionally.

Notes were put on several more neighbors' homes, however I received no further contacts. I did however speak to everyone close the Frashline home with the exception of Ms. Yount.

Database Search - Ms. Yount- Monday, August 24, 2009

I ran a name search and database and identified the subject as Ms. Merlynn Kay Yount SSN- 313-58-0493 DOB 8/27/1963 Address: 3130 Glenridge Drive, Palm Harbor, FL 34685-1723 Phone Number: 727.781.1836 (verified in name of Robert Yount)
Alt. Possible Number : 813.968.3055

I called both numbers above and left a brief message asking for a return call. I have not heard back from her as of this date.

Recorded Witness Statement
Nicholas Georges   Tuesday, August 25, 2009

I made a personal visit to Mr. George's address where he currently lives with his brother and another roommate while attending graduate school at UCF in Sociology. Mr. DeGeorge stated that he never meant to get involved in this situation. He stated that he believed Thomas Frashline injured his shoulder and it effected his ability to work and this was why he was fired from Belk's at the Tallahassee Mall. I asked him to clarify what the Plaintiffs attorney seemed to be representing by the statements. I asked him specifically if he felt the accident and the subsequent pain led to the claimant to committing suicide. He stated that he did not say that. He stated that he did not state that the injury or pain caused the suicide. He stated it was a combination of things, a combination of life's difficulties that Thomas struggled with. Thomas thought he would get his life on tract and thought he would get back together with Amber Anthony. He stated you know it is like the Romeo and Juliet effect he studied in Sociology. The witness stated that he took Thomas Frashline to work in the morning, picked him up for lunch and then picked him up to come home. He said Thomas depended on him and while he didn't see anything unusual about his personality, he knew he used drugs/marijuana regularly. The witness advised that he lived with Thomas for around six months before Thomas left to go care for his terminally ill father in NY or NJ. He then lived with him again when Amber Anthony brought him to Tallahassee. He stated that Thomas first started to work at a Cleaner's in Tallahassee, but had a conflict, he thinks it was with the hours they wanted him to work. He stated the claimant then went to Belks.

Mr. Georges stated that he does not know what has been represented by his statement to the Tallahassee Attorney, but he does not want to be involved. He lost a friend and that is it. He can not make any statement about any specific causation of the suicide. In fact, he stated that he gave multiple statements to the Attorney. Mr. Georges stated that he is joining the Military and will follow his brother's footsteps as he is currently serving in the Military. He will only speak the truth and has no agenda with this case nor does he want anyone to use or misrepresent his statements. In his statement he stated that the accident was like the straw that broke the camels back, but perhaps this has been misrepresented. Thomas had a lot of issues he was dealing with the most significant seemed to be his relationship with Ms. Angelo. Thomas felt, as did Georges, that they would get back together. Georges stated that he saw Thomas experience panic attacks when arguing with Ms. Angelo or hearing she was seeing another person. He stated he had no knowledge of Thomas' mental health or prior background and was not that close to him. He stated that he was actually closer to Thomas' brother. <u>He wanted to clearly state though that he never said nor meant to represent that the accident or pain Thomas felt from his injuries caused him to kill himself.</u>

Electronic Update   Wednesday, August 26, 2009

On the above date an electronic update/partial report was sent to the Claims Handler Mr. Steve Johnson and the SIU, Mr. Bill Howland. It appears the claimant became a highly depended person. He needed Amber Angelo to the point when things did not go well he developed panic attacks, threw up and couldn't sleep. The claimant reportedly had trouble sleeping but he also heavily used drugs/marijuana and also was believed to experiment with harder substances like acid. After his girlfriend could no longer handle the situation and dependency of the claimant she drove him to Tallahassee to live with Mr. Georges. The witness Georges described more of the same dependency. He drove the claimant to work, picked him up for lunch and at the end of the day. He too thought he could help the claimant get his life together. But he didn't know that the claimant may have had more serious issues as he knew nothing about his past and stated the claimant was a year older than him. He didn't even know if the claimant graduated from high school. Mr. Georges also confirmed the claimant used Marijuana regularly. Georges also knew that the claimant was supposed to go live with his mother in PA instead of coming to Tallahassee, but didn't recall what happened to change things. The witness, Ms. Angelo reported, she felt the mother knew what a problem Thomas was and didn't want anyone to know. In fact, Ms. Angelo believed Ms. Frashline probably knew Thomas needed medical attention or more serious help. Thomas suffered from Panic Attacks witnessed by Ms. Angelo and Mr. Georges. Panic attacks so severe that he threw up while working at Target. Neither, Ms. Angelo or Mr. Georges had a mental health background to diagnosis the causation or seriousness of the Mr. Frashline's situation. They both thought they could help Thomas, but perhaps they underestimated the severity of his mental health situation.

Internet Research Panic Attacks

Although the claimant's symptoms were referred to as Panic Attacks by the witnesses, they had no medical diagnosis. Ms. Angelo stated that Thomas would wake up in the middle of the night having the attack and would need to leave the house and walk around the block. To better understand this disorder, I conducted a brief search of the internet and found the The American Psychological Association states Panic Attacks are often experienced in conjunction with anxiety disorders and other psychological conditions, although panic attacks are not always indicative of a mental disorder, they have a multitude of causations. To name a few though I found it can be heredity, side effects from certain types of medications, or from various substances both prescribed and unprescribed as part of their withdrawal syndrome or rebound effect. Experiencing a panic attack is said to be one of the most intensely frightening, upsetting and uncomfortable experiences of a person's life (the claimant had them routinely). Sufferers of panic attacks often report a fear or sense of dying, "going crazy", or experiencing a heart attack or "flashing vision", feeling faint or nauseated (the claimant would throw up), heavy breathing, or losing control of themselves. These **feelings may provoke a strong urge to escape** or flee the place where the attack began (a consequence of the sympathetic "fight or flight" response).

This search made me wonder if the strong urge to escape could mean through suicide? If these attacks happened as often as described by the witnesses and were never treated professionaly how devastating could these episodes have been on his over all mental health?

Well, the question I raised also had an answer on the internet which I found at the following URL

http://sg.paniccenter.net/support/viewmessages.aspx?forum=35&topic=55200&ForumName=@NewForumName&TopicTitle=Topic:%20Did%20you%20know

Prolonged and untreated panic disorders can sometimes cause side effects like social anxiety, **depression**, and agoraphobia. Since panic attacks can occur during social situations, it can sometimes cause someone to develop performance anxiety or social anxiety. This is particularly true if the attacks frequently occur during times of great stress for the patient. Another possible reaction to these triggers can be depression and lack of confidence, as the person continues to fail in his endeavors. The onset of these side effects not only have an effect on mental health, but can also make recovery even more difficult. As such, it is critical that the problem be diagnosed and treated as early as possible. That way, the damage it can do is kept to a minimum.

I continued my search and found my questions were certainly not new and had been answered in a study published in The New England Journal of Medicine in November 1989, The link between Suicide and Panic Attacks or Panic Disorder

had long been recognized.
http://www.thefreelibrary.com/Panic+attacks+increase+suicide+attempts.-a08124445

New England Journal of Medicine November 2
Excerpt from Article:

Some psychiatric conditions, such as severe depression and schizophrenia, are known to increase a person's risk of suicide. But panic attacks and <u>panic disorder</u> defined as frequently recurring panic attacks, are also linked to a strong and largely unappreciated risk of contemplating and attempting suicide according to a new study. Surprisingly, people with panic disorder have a higher rate of suicide attempts than do severely depressed individuals, report psychologist Myrna M. Weissman of <u>Columbia University</u>

This finding is "quite remarkable" **<u>and marks panic disorder as a major new risk factor for suicide,</u>** *writes psychiatrist Peter Reich of the <u>Massachusetts Institute of Technology</u> Cambridge in an editorial in the same journal. Reich also notes that general practice physicians, who most commonly encounter panic disorder patients, <u>can help prevent suicides by recognizing and treating symptoms of the disorder.</u>*

This case continued as I followed up on other leads and details provided. The end result however indicated that his suicide was more likely associated to his drug use and mental health problems than a car accident.

Insurance Cases

SIU investigations refer to general investigations about most any type of claim that needs to be investigated and usually does not require any type of surveillance. These types of cases require good interviewing skills and analysis of the evidence to determine the cause or origin of an accident/incident. If someone slipped and fell in a supermarket, you would investigate what caused the fall, could it have been prevented? What can be done to prevent the fall from occurring again and was it a realistic accident. By realistic, I mean how often does this type of accident occur? Could it be that the person simply just tripped or slipped? Could it just have been their worn leather soles or a loose flip flop? In investigating an accident you need to look for any ambiguity with the accident. Proving or disproving the likeliness of the accident will take documentation. Is there any store video that shows the incident as it took place? Gather facts and statistics that may also cast some doubt on the incident actually being a liable accident. Accidents occur all the time but those that occur due to a problematic situation are those were liability may occur and thus damages may be brought against the property owner. With statistics, you may find that the store has over 200 register receipts daily and at a minimum, this would mean 200 people may walk through the same door or over the same threshold one customer tripped over. You may photograph the threshold and find it flush and without any obstruction which could have contributed to the fall. Secondly, I might speak or take statements from several patrons of the store in the parking lot after they have departed the store. I may look for an elderly woman or one using a cane and attempt to obtain a quick statement from her asking how many times a week she visits the store and for how many years she has been coming. I would then specifically ask her if she ever tripped in the area of the accident location. Obviously I am hoping to hear, "I have been coming to this store for 25 years and have had a hip replacement and use a cane. I usually come to the store twice a week and exit through those doors each time and have never tripped or ever felt the exit was dangerous or presented a hazard." I then ask if I can just take a quick picture, hold up my phone and snap her picture. During the statement I would have also asked the woman her name. The good thing about a parking lot is that I can see her walk tot her car and also get the tag to her car which will further give me her address.

Thinking on your feet on how to approach an investigation will vary from case to case. I was assigned a case where a hotel guest stated that the shower head shot off and hit him in the head while he was showering. I started by meeting the maintenance man and getting a full description of the type of shower heads he uses and any maintenance records for that specific hotel room. I then asked for access to the specific room with the original head that allegedly shot off and hit the subject. I took my video camera and set it up to record an attempt to duplicate the incident. I screwed on the shower head and turned the water on full force. With my video recording, I turned the shower head a half rotation off until final the shower head was being held on by just one thread. Water was spraying everywhere and finally as the last thread was loosened the head just dropped straight down into the tub. There was no pressure or force that could have turned the shower head in a dangerous projectile as described by the guest. I also secured a statement from the maintenance man about any similar accident of course finding that there had been none. I also photographed the threads of the shower water spout as well as the threads on the shower head itself to show they were not worn or damaged. I then confiscated the shower head itself as an evidence item. My final report determined that the accident could not have occurred as alleged.

Staged fraudulent claims and exaggerated claims of injuries purporting a libelous situation are the types of jobs we see most frequently from the insurance industry.

We can also investigate thefts, homeowner burglaries, auto thefts and even fires.

Sometimes we conduct parallel investigations acting as the middle man to gather information. In the case of a suspected arson, the fire marshal's office may be investigating the incident with a full staff of professional cause and origin experts. They may clearly feel it was an arson, but are under no specific time frame to complete their investigation and produce a report. On the other hand though, the property owner may want to be paid for his loss so that he can rebuild or re-locate. They may even want a per diem so that they can stay in a hotel while the insurance company processes the claim. The adjuster with the insurance company is on a tight time-line, but she cannot control the fire departments investigation. But the Professional PI should be able to introduce himself as an agent of the insurance company to get a feel for the direction of the investigation. If the Fire Department states this was and arson set fire then the case may quickly turn to who set the fire and why. A motive to set a car, house or business fire usually first falls on the owner. This is an investigation well within the scope and capabilities of any PI. Was the

owner behind in his payments, was he/she having financial problems? Was there a problem with the business, was it failing. Was the car having mechanical difficulties or the home involved in a contested nasty divorce or the owners underwater in the evaluation of the property. If the fire was NOT an arson but a fire that started due to some faulty electrical work in a back addition, then the investigation may shift from a parallel gathering informational investigation to an active self directed investigation. The PI will want to know who did the electrical work in the addition as this party may be at fault for the loss. The PI will search for the building permits identifying the electrician. If there were no permits pulled and no plans or building inspections made then the work may have been done illegally and improper. Insurance companies do not cover illegal acts and the fire damage may not be covered.

When investigating a homeowner burglary, we usually meet with the home owner, pick up a copy of the police report and look for the forced entry point. We cover each item stolen, where it was located, what brand it was and ask for any of the accessories that may go with the item such as a manual, remote control or to see pictures with the items in the background or being worn by the subject if it was jewelry. We are always trying to verify the validity of a claim. Ironically, I have investigated many homeowner burglaries and each time a TV set is reported as stolen, it is always described as a "Sony". If a fur coat is taken from the closet, it is always a "Blue Fox". I always ask to see where the coat was hanging in the closet and take a picture of the closet. Many times the closets are so full there isn't even room for a thick bulky fur. This is when I ask for pictures of the subject wearing the coat. If a video camera is stolen, I ask to see the box, the manual, the remote. Same holds true for a TV. I ask to see pictures of the same room with the TV present. Once again, there may be a financial motive for the owners of the property to have made the claim or loss. Some of the items may have been financed and the owners currently unable to make payments. There may have been a split in the household, two roommates leave and one takes property the other wanted or the property was taken by a family member or friends and the owner feels reporting it stolen is an easier way to handle the situation.

Whatever type of investigation you may be called to conduct chances are someone has worked a similar case before. Outlines of what to do and what to look for are prevalent within our industry.

Domestic / Infidelity Investigations

Our industry has a wide range of avenues to specialize in; perhaps the most prolific for small start-up agencies are Domestic Investigations, specifically Infidelity. The most successful agencies will learn to Flat Rate their pricing which is still lagging in the industry. As indicated I would suggest packaging surveillance 5 hours at a time ($250.00) and elicit the assistance of the client spouse. Next, creating a "window of opportunity" is the best approach to saving time. Have the spouse you are working for tell the significant other that they need to be out of town for work leaving at 6:00 p.m. and most likely being back the following morning. The significant other can also state they are going to help a friend move or assist a sick family member.  What ever the case, the destination needs to be at least three hours away and the spouse needs to call the other spouse right when they leave and again when they get to their destination. I suggest leaving at 2:00 p.m. - 3:00 p.m. so by 5:00 p.m. you are three hours away. Meanwhile, the PI is on the suspected cheater and having this window of opportunity is just too tempting to resist. If the spouse does not use the time period to see the other party then the relationship has probably been discontinued. If the client believes otherwise suggest doing the same thing on another weekend.

Forensic Computer Investigations

Is another increasing specialized area of practice and also another "Flat Rate" opportunity to secure business. The client spouse can authorize the PI to forensically examine the computer or even install a key tracking software that will capture all correspondence, usually for a home visit of around $199.00. Statistics shows that 22 percent of men and 14 percent of women admitted to having sexual relations outside their marriage sometime in their past. And 17 percent of divorces in the United States are caused by infidelity. Results show that internet users devote three hours each week to online sexual exploits. Twenty-five percent have felt that they lost control of their Internet sexual exploits at least once or that the activity caused problems in their lives. Researchers think the vast majority of the millions of people who visit chat rooms, have multiple "special friends" and only 46% of men believe that online affairs are adultery. According to Divorce Magazine 80% think it's Ok to talk with a stranger identified as the opposite sex.

It is currently estimated that <u>one-third of divorce litigation is caused by online affairs.</u>

Because of the anonymity, affordability, and accessibility of Internet sexual resources, the computer can accelerate relationships. 57% of people have used the Internet to flirt. 38% of people have engaged in explicit online sexual conversation and 50% of people have made phone contact with someone they chatted with online.

The professional PI can utilize special industry strength software and hardware to retrieve the truth from any computer. This software can be easily loaded on a thumb drive for an at home visit by a field investigator.

A product called PC PANDORA http://www.pcpandora.com is a PC and Internet detective that hides on a hard drive and monitors all computer and Internet activity. This program will record and take snapshots of the websites visited, emails sent and received, Instant Messages sent and received, Chat room conversions and other computer and Internet activity that is done on a clients PC. This software can also be used as a key logger that will record secret passwords that someone may want to keep hidden. Once known they can be used to access other accounts on Hotmail, YAHOO, AOL or other web based email accounts. This is just one internet detective program that comes to mind and more sophisticated programs are developed all the time. You should consultant an expert in the field before deciding which to buy.

Other Domestic Investigations involve background checks on couples, renters, business partners and disputes between neighbors. Others may choose to support the corporate Human Resource industry and handle work related incidents such as conducting pre-hiring background checks, sexual harassment allegations, internal security and theft just to name a few.

Another large market that requires a very professional approach and preparation is to specialize in insurance related issues sometime overlapping with the aforementioned corporate investigators with the addition of some of the biggest accounts in our industry; Workers Compensation and General Liability Claims. Another avenue is to work directly for the Insurance Companies as a staff investigator in the Special Investigative Unit SIU, investigating auto, property and liability claims both personal and commercial Lines.

Then there are jobs with Criminal and Civil Defense Attorneys, seeking to provide a defense for their clients. It is very common for the PI to secure statements, locate witnesses and take pictures of an accident location to assist in the defense of the client.

Chapter Twelve
Being a Witness

 I. Deposition Testimony
 II. Courtroom Testimony
 III. Being a Witness is Serious Business
 IV. Do's and Don'ts of Testifying in Court or Deposition

12. You've Been Served a Subpoena: Don't Panic

You've been served a subpoena to appear and testify in a lawsuit which you investigated or are a part of but not a party. The subpoena may direct you to appear at a law office to give deposition testimony or may direct you to appear in court to give trial testimony, and may request that you bring certain documents with you such as you report, notes surveillance tapes, photographs etc. In either event, you are upset that someone (sometimes a sheriff) has appeared at your home or workplace with a subpoena and apprehensive about what will be expected of you when testifying. You  recall very little about the case and need to pull the file and refresh your memory, never just trust your recollection.

You should understand that the party calling you as a witness was required by law to serve you with a subpoena to assure your appearance and testimony. Service of the subpoena was not designed to embarrass you, but protect the parties to the lawsuit.

If you have questions about the subpoena, the scheduling of your testimony or the underlying litigation, you should speak to your office manager or sponsor. Always immediately notify the office and your manager. Your manager will next instruct to contact the client and determine who the attorney is on your client file. This attorney will be present during your deposition and will most likely want to meet with you before the deposition to go over your testimony.

Deposition Testimony

Witnesses are frequently asked to testify twice in connection with a single matter. The first time you testify may be on deposition. Deposition testimony is typically given in a conference room setting rather than in a courtroom. The purpose of a deposition is to find out what you know about the case. The lawyers for the parties, possibly the parties themselves, and a court reporter will be present.

You will take an oath to tell the truth. The court reporter will record all the questions asked by the lawyers and all responses given by you. The deposition may be taken many months or even years before the case is actually tried. The purpose of the deposition testimony is to record your recollections of the events at a time when they are relatively fresh in your mind. Afterward, testimony will be typed in a deposition transcript after it is given, and you will be given the opportunity to read and sign it. If you are at all concerned that the court reporter may have improperly recorded your testimony, you should exercise your right to read and sign the transcript and correct those areas in the transcript where your testimony is incorrectly recorded.

Courtroom Testimony

The second time you testify may be in a courtroom before a judge and possibly, a jury. You may wonder why you have to testify a second time when you have already given your deposition testimony. You should understand that the judge and jurors were not present when you gave your deposition testimony. In most instances the rules of court forbid the use of your deposition without the use of your live testimony. Remember that the lawyers investigate the case thoroughly and know what testimony they must present. If they judge your testimony to be essential, they will call you. Otherwise, you will not receive a subpoena.

Being a Witness is Serious Business

Remember that your role as a witness in the judicial system is an extremely important one. Without witnesses, judges, and jurors could not fairly decide cases. Never be argumentative or combative, with the plaintiff's attorney. He/She will do their best to get under you skin but listen carefully and answer to the best of your ability. Use your best efforts to present a clear and accurate answer.

DO's and DON'Ts for Testifying in Court or Deposition

1. Do go over the facts of the case in your mind prior to testifying. Separate what you remember from what you think you remember. You should always review with the lawyer who intends to call you as a witness.
2. Do answer as truthfully, accurately and completely as possible. Don't answer a question with half-truths or let your judgment about how the case should come out affect your testimony. Remember that you took an oath before testifying to tell the truth. A failure to tell the truth amounts to perjury.
3. Do correct any mistakes made in answering a question immediately.
4. Do speak slowly and loudly so that all concerned can hear your testimony.
5. Do dress neatly and dress professionally.
6. Do make estimations if a question requires you to do so, but be clear in your answer that your testimony is only an estimate.

7. If you were asked whether you have discussed your testimony with others before testifying if in fact you have. There is absolutely nothing wrong with discussing your testimony with lawyers or parties beforehand.
8. Do take a <u>subpoena</u> seriously. It has the force of a court order. That doesn't mean, by the way, that a judge has actually taken an interest in you (they are usually prepared by an attorney for a party) but a judge will be annoyed if you ignore a subpoena.
9. Do be honest and forthcoming with your testimony. That doesn't mean spill your guts out, but answer questions fairly and with intellectual honesty. You saw how badly a recent President looked when he tried to get cute with his testimony. Of course, also remember that perjury is a felony.
10. Do be honest and forthcoming with your attorney. Even if it is embarrassing, even if it makes you look like an idiot or a crook, it is better if your attorney knows. Giving your attorney insufficient information is like hiring a chauffeur and not telling him or her that your brakes don't work.
11. Do make yourself available to your attorney for discussions regarding the case, including working on discovery and preparation for depositions and trial. It is not a waste of your time if it helps you to win the lawsuit.
12. Do follow your attorney's advice about how to behave in the deposition or the courtroom. Don't be afraid to ask him or her if something is appropriate. It's one of the things that you are paying your lawyer for. Your attorney will tell you what he or she wants from you if you are deposed or have to take the stand in a trial.
13. Do dress as well as you comfortably can. A suit is best, for a man or a woman, but if your head spins and you gag at the thought of a tie or a skirt, dress as nicely as you can. If you are a police officer, military personnel, or cleric, your uniform is always appropriate. Your credibility as a witness is in some small degree judged by your clothing.
14. Do give your attorney everything in your relevant files, even if it is embarrassing or incriminating. If you have the document, the odds are that someone else does too.

THE DON'Ts

15. Don't attempt to answer a question unless you fully understand it. Ask the lawyer to rephrase the question. Don't guess at what you think the lawyer is after, make the lawyer explain the question to you.
16. Don't try to respond to a question if you don't know the answer. If you don't remember or know the answer to a question, say so.
17. Don't attempt to answer a question to which an objection has been made. When a lawyer makes an objection or the judge makes a comment, stop talking. Wait for a ruling by the judge. If he overrules the objection, you should answer the question. Listen to each objection made, so that you understand the basis for the objection.
18. Don't argue with the lawyers or the judge. Don't allow them to make you angry. Be cool, calm and attentive.

19. Don't guess. It is okay to provide a reasoned or thoughtful estimate, but do not simply guess or speculate as to an answer.
20. Don't be offended if you are told not to listen to testimony given by other witnesses in the case. There is an important reason for this rule. No one wants your testimony to be colored by the testimony of other witnesses. You will be expected to give your version of what happened rather than to parrot someone else's version.
21. Don't ever guess. You are in a deposition or on the stand to give facts, not to try to figure out what might have happened. Even if it makes you feel stupid to say it, sometimes "I don't know" is the right answer.
22. Don't help. It is human nature to want to explain things so that your listener understands. Resist the impulse. It is your opponent's job to get the answers. It is your job to answer only the question asked, and not help.
23. Don't try to be funny, unless you are actually Jerry Seinfeld. There are several reasons for not even trying. First, and most obviously, not everyone has the same sense of humor; some people, and there are judges in this category, have no humor at all. Second, your words are taken down by a court reporter to be read later. The court reporter does not take down facial expressions, gestures, or tones of voice. You can be saying "yes" in a sarcastic whiny voice while making quote marks with your fingers, and what will appear on the page is "Yes."
24. Don't get distracted. Pay strict and guarded attention to the questions being asked. If your attention wanders, you could make mistakes or misunderstand.
25. Don't answer a question you don't understand. If a question is vague or compound ("Did you go to the store and who did you see and what did you say to them?") or assumes something that isn't true, you have the right to have the question restated or rephrased.
26. Don't be afraid to ask for a break during a deposition. They can take hours, and it is inhumane to expect you to sit and squirm if you need a restroom break. BUT-
27. Don't' even think of asking for a break while you are at trial. Breaks are entirely in the control of the judge, and asking for a break (unless something dreadful happens, like you start crying) looks very bad.
28. Don't take any drugs or alcohol before you testify. This may seem obvious, but you'd be surprised. Remember that "drugs" also includes things like cold medicine, or even more caffeine than you are used to. You should also be careful what you eat before you testify. That isn't the morning to skip breakfast if you usually have it.

Chapter Thirteen
Terrorism Today

      I.   Introduction
      II.   Private Investigators and Terrorism
      III.   Different Types of Terrorism
      IV.   How to Report Terrorism Activity

13. Introduction

Terrorism may be something we will need to live with for many decades to come. The reasons behind terrorism associated with attacks on America and American Ideology is a vast topic for discussion. There are varying types of terrorism such as those home-grown related to idealistic thoughts, those related to religious radicals and finally those associated to purely pathological thinking.

I consider the Columbine and Sandy Hook shootings acts of terror from pathological disorders. I would argue that anyone involved in a terrorist act has some type of pathological disorder. After all, acts of terror are crimes, and we associate most criminal behavior with deviant or pathological disorders.

What causes a religious person to become radicalized to the point that they want to hurt innocent people has less to do with religion than it does to their own personal situation.

Many areas of the middle-east lack the social and religious freedoms more advanced societies enjoy. In a suppressed environment personal growth and educational opportunities can be stifled. Feelings of hopelessness associated with no opportunity to advance their personal or family's financial well-being can be the formula for feelings of resentment or even hatred. People tend to look towards religion in times of personal distress. If you cannot control your own environment or circumstances often people tend to look towards their faith for guidance. When I lost my job in 1997, I made sure I didn't miss church on Sundays. There are many misguided and demented so-called leaders of groups of other misguided followers. Some of these deviants operate under the cloke of a religious organization trying to justify their promise or message by high-jacking a religious theme. There will always be groups and leaders that feel their circumstances are more tragic than others. Or they are created through nothing but greed. We don't need to go far from home to find examples of this. The Reverend Jim Jones started the Peoples Temple to help homeless, jobless and sick people of all races. When former members claimed widespread abuse within the group, Jones started a colony in the jungles of Guyana, where he hoped to build a tropical utopia. When a congressman visited the commune with three journalists to investigate the abuse claims, they were shot and killed when trying to leave. After the shootings, 913 commune members, including hundreds of children drank poisoned cool aid. Then we have David Koresh (born Vernon Wayne Howell) the convicted leader of the Branch Davidiians who raped girls as young as 12 years old. And finally more recently, Warren Jeff's of the Fundamentalist Church of Jesus Christ of Latter-Day Saints who was found guilty of sexual assault and aggravated sexual assault of children. Jeffs was sentenced to life in prison plus 20 years, to be served consecutively for sexual assault of both 12- and 15-year-old girls.

Radicalization can be defined as an opinion that differs from that of the moderate and most generally accepted. But sometimes these views and the way they are delivered can affect a person more differently depending on his or her situation. Mental Health is such a complex area of study that even the most advanced counties in the world including the US struggle to implement ways to identify it, treat it, manage it and un-stignafy it.

So pathologic leaders can convince mis directed people to do outrageous things including killing.

In the Boston Bombings the Tsarnev brothers became radicalized, perhaps through different methods but if we consider where they came from and perhaps what happened to them later we may find failures and feelings of frustration in their lives, Specifically the older Tsarnev who may have felt the frustration of not having the same opportunities as others, he faced problems with education, he wanted to be an Olympic Boxer and failed. He sought US citizenship and was denied. These failures and frustration combined with perhaps his own feelings of inadequacy and underlying psychological problems created a person ready to be used by another deviant misguided leader.

In most cases the people caught up in these types of horrendous circumstances lack their own defined purpose or ideas. Many people that join the military join because it is an option in an otherwise option-less path. People join militias of all types including what we call terrorist groups. Many of these kids have no other group to join or associate with. They have no personal path, no ideas or objectives of their own. They band together with other hooligans and are accepted into a group that feeds them, houses them creates a sense of brotherhood, set out to fight for a cause that in most cases is nothing more than a misconceived ideology by some radical unstable thinker.

Professor Falk, who teaches at UC-Santa Barbara, called the Boston victims "canaries" and suggested that the U.S. had it coming because of our geopolitical fantasy of global domination. I would be concerned about even stepping foot in one of his classes as he clearly doesn't understand the complexity of America. While we may use drones and intervene in tumultuous situations around the world, we don't plant out flag, we try to organize a stable government with people of that country. The US then works on an exit strategy to leave that country a more democrat and humanistic society.

The United States has always been a melting pot of cultures. It wasn't to long ago that the Irish and Italians came here and wanted help in their countries civil un-rest. Today's Iranian Americans, Iraqi Americans all have family members or relative back home that may still live under harsh conditions or suppressed human rights. Having the privilege of being an American, they feel it is their duty to do what they can to help those left behind. With a wife who is from Colombia, I know she would support any US policy that helps rid her homeland of drug trafficking. I see our presence in Colombia fighting narco-trafficking and corruption no different than helping free the Iraqi people from radical islamists.

I recently took a trip to Morocco which of its approximate 33 million people, 99.9 percent are Muslims. My Muslim driver who spent his off-time raising sheep stated that the younger population is being educated through satellite TV and the dishes could be seen on the roof tops of almost every single house in each village we passed. With the average wage of a Moroccan only $9.00 US dollars a day, higher education is expensive and not affordable to most. It may just be though those satellite dishes the younger generation is enabled to connect to the rest of the world. Without such a connection, they have no idea to really understand what is happening around the rest of the world. In a place so large with so many people, I was amazed at the daily call for pray ringing out over loud speaker strategically located throughout the town. People would make their way to the Mosques for prayer. While I think religion is important, this type of daily repetitive religious beating seemed almost like brain washing to me.

So, I say thank god for satellite dishes that bring the world to those who may be stranded elsewhere. Sane, socially adjusted, educated people don't become radicals. Any way we can promote tolerance and education will be ultimately good for the world. I tend to want to believe that as an American society our leaders ultimately want to do the right thing and are largely swayed by their constituents whether individuals or large businesses. Do we get things wrong or are we too ambitious sometimes to see the pitfalls of our efforts, sure, but we are a nation of people and people aren't perfect. Regardless of our critics homegrown or abroad, I don't see global domination by the US. Rather I see an interest to pursue democracy and freedom for global regions that have an impact on the US or raise a concern to those empowered to invoke change that supports humane and civil rights for all mankind.

Private Investigators and Terrorism

The purpose of this chapter might not initially be obvious however in early 2000, the State Department and now the Department of Homeland Security recognized that there was an invaluable civilian army of eyes around the country. With approximately 9,000 Private Investigators in Florida, 60,000 nationwide, working the streets daily, making sure they realize the importance of their trained eyes can only add to the protection of our country and its' citizens. Unfortunately in this day and age, forces are at work around us to undermine the safety of our nation. The most notorious of these groups today is Al-Qaeda and their related organizations. With such an open society the ways in which a terrorist group might strike is abundant.

Al-Qaeda

The radical Islamist movement developed during the Islamic revival and Islamist movement of the last three decades of the 20th century, along with less extreme movements.

Some have argued that "without the writings" of Islamic author and thinker Sayyid Qutb, "al-Qaeda would not have existed."Qutb preached that because of the lack of *sharia* law, the Muslim world was no longer Muslim, having reverted to pre-Islamic ignorance known as *jahiliyyah*.

To restore Islam, he said a movement of righteous Muslims was needed to establish "true Islamic states", implement *sharia*, and rid the Muslim world of any non-Muslim influences, such as concepts like socialism and nationalism.

Hamas (Islamic Resistance Movement)

Hamas was formed in late 1987 as an outgrowth of the Palestinian branch of the Muslim Brotherhood. Various Hamas elements have used both violent and political means, including terrorism, to pursue the goal of establishing an Islamic Palestinian state in Israel. It is loosely structured, with some elements working clandestinely and others operating openly through mosques and social service institutions to recruit members, raise money, organize activities, and distribute propaganda. Hamas' strength is concentrated in the Gaza Strip and the West Bank.

Hamas currently limits its terrorist operations to Israeli military and civilian targets in the West Bank, Gaza Strip, and Israel. The terrorist group receives some funding from Iran but primarily relies on donations from Palestinian expatriates around the world and private benefactors in Saudi Arabia and other Arab states. Some fundraising and propaganda activity take place in Western Europe and North America.

Different Types of Terrorism

Researchers in the United States began to distinguish different types of terrorism in the 1970s, following a decade in which both domestic and international groups flourished. By that point, modern groups had began to use techniques such as hijacking, bombing, diplomatic kidnapping and assassination to assert their demands and, for the first time, they appeared as real threats to Western democracies, in the view of politicians, law makers, law enforcement and researchers. They began to distinguish different types of terrorism as part of the larger effort to understand how to counter and deter it.

State Terrorism

Many definitions of terrorism restrict it to acts by non-state actors. But it can also be argued that states can, and have, been terrorists. States can use force or the threat of force, without declaring war, to terrorize citizens and achieve a political goal. Germany under Nazi rule has been described in this way.

It has also been argued that states participate in international terrorism, often by proxy. The United States considers Iran the most prolific sponsor of terrorism because Iran arms groups, such as Hezbollah, that help carry out its foreign policy objectives.

Bioterrorism

Bioterrorism refers to the intentional release of toxic biological agents to harm and terrorize civilians, in the name of a political or other cause. The U.S. Center for Disease Control has classified the viruses, bacteria and toxins that could be used in an attack. Category A Biological Diseases are those most likely to do the most damage. They include Anthrax, Botulism, The Plague, Smallpox, Tularemia and Hemorrhagic fever, due to Ebola Virus or Marburg Virus.

Cyberterrorism

Cyberterrorists use information technology to attack civilians and draw attention to their cause. This may mean that they use information technology, such as computer systems or telecommunications, as a tool to orchestrate a traditional attack. More often, cyberterrorism refers to an attack on information technology itself in a way that would radically disrupt networked services. For example, cyberterrorists could disable networked emergency systems or hack into networks housing critical financial information. There is wide disagreement over the extent of the existing threat by cyberterrorists.

Ecoterrorism

Ecoterrorism is a recently coined term describing violence in the interests of environmentalism. In general, environmental extremists sabotage property to inflict economic damage on industries or actors they see as harming animals or the natural environment. These have included fur companies, logging companies and animal research laboratories, for example.

Nuclear terrorism

"Nuclear terrorism" refers to a number of different ways nuclear materials might be exploited as a terrorist tactic. These include attacking nuclear facilities, purchasing nuclear weapons, or building nuclear weapons or otherwise finding ways to disperse radioactive materials.

Narcoterrorism

Narcoterrorism has had several meanings since its coining in 1983. It once denoted violence used by drug traffickers to influence governments or prevent government efforts to stop the drug trade. In the last several years, Narcoterrorism has been used to indicate situations in which terrorist groups use drug trafficking to fund their other operations.

How to Report Suspected Terrorist Activity

Terrorist are constantly plotting and while we never know when they might strike, the safety of our people is our government's highest priority. As a group of Professional Investigators and Security Specialists keep an eye out for suspicious behavior or things out of place. Use your trained investigative eye and make note. Or act immediately by calling the local police department.

Take the following steps:

- Note as many physical characteristics of the person or persons involved in the suspicious event as possible. Report the suspicious party's sex, race, approximate age, height and weight, clothing, hair color and distinguishing characteristics (tattoos, accent, scars, facial hair and other identifying marks).
- Describe in detail exactly what you saw during the suspicious event. Know the time, location, what happened, who was involved and in what direction the suspects left. Your eyewitness account can aid law enforcement officials' efforts to apprehend the suspects. Take detailed notes of what you saw.
- Note characteristics of any vehicle the suspects used to make a getaway. The make, model, year, color, license plate number and any distinctive characteristics (dents, bumper stickers, tinted glass or paint chips) are all

important details that can help law enforcement officials hunt the car down.
- Report peculiar incidents to your local police using their non-emergency number. Have your description of the suspects and notes regarding the incident ready. You may be asked to give your name and address. Remember that you are under no obligation to provide your personal information, although this may help law enforcement if they have further questions.
- Inform the Federal Bureau of Investigation of the suspicious incident. You can submit a tip by telephone, or anonymously, on their Web site (see Resources below). This contact information can also be found on the front cover of your local telephone directory.
- Call 911 only in an emergency situation. 911 is not the most effective source of help in cases of suspected terrorist activity which are not immediately life-threatening. However, suspicious unattended vehicles or packages left in public places may represent extreme public danger. Consider such a situation to be an emergency requiring the immediate attention of law enforcement officials.

Chapter Fourteen
Statement Taking

I. Introduction
II. Recorded Statement Format
III. Written Statement Format
IV. Principles of Interviewing
V. Interviewing Do's
VI. Interviewing Don'ts
VII. Getting Started
VIII. Written or Recorded
IX. Over-the-phone or In Person
X. Sample Report
XI. Formats

14. Preparing for the Statement

I. Introduction

Before going out, make sure you have a clear understanding of your objective. You can't conduct a thorough interview if all you ask is what happened, who was injured, and who or what was responsible.

Knowing and understanding the reason for the statement is the key. A client may ask for a statement simply to document their file. However, their purpose may be to determine liability, subrogation, for an uninsured motorist claim, for a PIP claim, to determine compensability or a pre-existing condition. There are a host of other reasons but these cover primarily why we would be taking a statement. The following are a few examples of why one would be taking a statement in a particular type of claim.

Auto:

Liability--Subrogation--Uninsured Motorist--Wrongful Death--PIP

Workers' Compensation:

Compensability--Subrogation--Pre-exiting Condition

Slip and Fall:

Liability and Subrogation

Medical Malpractice:

Liability

Food Poisoning:

Liability

Fire and Arson:

Motive (assets)--Point of Origin--Flammables--Property Damage

Auto Theft:

Keys--Financial, Mechanical Problems

Theft:

Property Loss--Forced Entry--Property Damage Loss List

PREPARATION

Review your assignment and locate a good "base" outline appropriate to the type of claim. Have a note pad and diagram sheet available. Make your own list of questions as well.

All Statements will follow the basic format with an INTRODUCTION; BODY OF STATEMENT (questions); and a CLOSING (refer to following page for example).

PLAN AND CONTROL

Carefully plan the conversation, briefly outline your approach. Take notes, during the conversation. Listen to the interviewee's responses. Their responses should prompt additional clarification questions. Remember, anyone listening to or reading the transcription from a recorded statement should have enough information to understand the incident or accident being explored.

INFORMALITY

Remember to use an informal positive approach. If you want a person to be your friend, treat him as if he is your friend; if you want a recorded statement, treat him as if he will give you one.

REVIEW

Review the assignment and have all known facts well fixed in your mind.

COURTESY

Remember -- courtesy is essential.

II. Recorded Statement Format

(Turn Recorder On)

Today's date is (date). My name is (your name). I am employed with Claims Resource Incorporated., Orlando, Florida and I am representing (name of Client Company). I am at (the location where you are taking statement).

I am interviewing (name of subject) who was (involved in the accident, witnessed, etc.). (Name of person) Are you aware that I am recording our conversation? (Response) Do I have your permission to do so? (Response)

BODY OF STATEMENT

Depending on type of statement, refer to statement outlines and your own prepared notes and questions. Address the specific concerns of the client, such as any special questions indicated on the assignment sheet that must be covered. Be certain that you fully cover and understand how the incident or accident occurred. This should be a relaxed conversation so put your interviewee and your self at ease. Don't be afraid to ask questions out of order. If a question comes to mind ask it. You can rarely ask too many questions.

CLOSING

Ask:

Is there anything else you would like to add or clarify in this statement before I conclude the recording? (Response). (If response is no) . . . If there is nothing else, I will conclude this statement.

(Subject's name) were you aware that I was recording our conversation? (If the response is no, proceed with closing; If the response is yes, let the subject explain and ask follow up questions if necessary. Once you are through, repeat this statement again before proceeding.) (Subject's Name) Were you aware I was recording our conversation? (Response)) Did I have your permission to do so? (Response) (Subject's Name) Was everything you told me true and correct to the best of your knowledge and belief? (Response) Would you please statement your name for the final time. My name is (Your Name). Thank you for voluntarily giving this statement. (Turn Recorder Off).

NOTE

When taking a statement, avoid turning the recorder off once statement is started. If you do, you must say why the recorder is being turned off. When you turn it back on, you need to state that you are continuing with the recording and identify person and self again.

III. Written Statement Format

The most obvious difference between the two will be the means in which the statement is taken. Be ready to write for an extended length of time so find a comfortable writing position at a desk or table.

Make certain you are using the carbonless, three part lined statement paper. This paper is available in each branch office. The top original white copy will be sent to the client with your report. The next yellow copy will be stapled to your notes and the third part should be handed to the person whom the statement was taken from.

Fill in date, place of taking, and page number of statement in upper right hand corner.

The written statement should be taken as if the person wrote it themselves. You should however write the statement so that all vital questions are answered. Also, by the investigator writing the statement, the handwriting should be legible. The written statement should a continuous narrative without any paragraphs or blank spaces. If you make a mistake both parties should initial the correction. Below is an example of how the statement should be written.

Example:

    My name is Veronica M. Brown and I am here today this 10th day of June with James Corn of Claims Resource Incorporated. We are here today in regards to the automobile accident, slip and fall, stolen property, etc., which occurred on (date) and (location). I am a 25 years old white female, born on July 7, 1965. I currently reside at 1276 Deer Lake Circle, Apopka, Florida 32712. My telephone number is 904-896-4629. I am married to Tim Brown who presently works for All American Gym as the manager (additional witness identification information). On the afternoon at approximately 2:30 p.m., I was driving home from having just picked my husband up from work. I was driving our 1993 blue Plymouth Voyager while my husband was seated on the passenger's side when he yelled look out! Just then I slammed on my breaks and skidded approximately 20 feet. We were both wearing our seat belts and I was only driving at approximately 45 mph so we stopped in time. The road was dry and it was a clear day. Since my husband was on the passenger side and staring out the passenger side window, he noticed a stampeding bull headed right for the road in from of us. We were driving on Old Winter Garden road heading south and my husband was starring east. The guy behind us had been tail gating me for about 5 miles ever since I left the gym. At about five miles on Old Winter Garden Road, the area gets real rural and I guess he felt it was a good place to pass. The guy who was passing me must have been looking for any oncoming cars because he sure didn't see that bull coming etc...

Remember as this hypothetical example exhibits, each line should be continuous without any large spaces. This will prevent any room to alter or add information to the final statement that was not intended to be part of the statement. Whenever any corrections or error is made, be sure to have the interviewee initial the corrections. Number each page by using "Page 1 of 3; Page 2 of 3; Page 3 of 3", etc.

CLOSING

Have the interviewee initial each page.

Ask the subject whether there is anything else they would like to say with regards to this incident. Write exactly what they say. If they have nothing else to say, close with the following final statement and the interviewee's signature.

> "I have read the above statement of _____ pages and it is true and correct to the best of my knowledge and belief." X_____ (Signature of Interviewee)

Detach the last (pink) copy of the three part statement paper and provide the interviewee with a complete copy of his written statement.

IV. Principles of Interviewing

INTERVIEWING   is a <u>specialized</u> way of asking questions.

INTERVIEWING   is the art of extracting the <u>maximum</u> amount of <u>truthful</u> information from an individual.

INTERVIEW   is the questioning of a person who is believed to possess knowledge that is of official interest to the investigator.

    An <u>INTERVIEW</u> is conducted for the purpose of gaining information that may establish the facts of an accident or incident and that may provide the investigator with leads which will further substantiate the validity of the claim.

    In an <u>INTERVIEW</u> (claimants, witnesses, employers, supervisors, co-workers, etc.) the interviewee usually gives his account of the accident/incident in his own words and in his own way.

    In an <u>INTERVIEW</u>, a specialized way and/or technique is used in asking questions.

WITNESS   one who has <u>seen</u> or <u>knows</u> something concerning the incident under investigation and is competent of discussing it.

6 - Basic questions which must be exploited to the maximum in every interview.

WHO?
WHAT?
WHEN?
WHERE?
WHY?
HOW?

V. Interviewing Do's

1. DO provide a suitable place for the interview.
2. DO fix the time for the interview, if possible.
3. DO have the witness conform to your arrangements, if possible.
4. DO show some consideration for the witness, once he indicates that he is cooperating.
5. DO seat the witness and place him at ease.
6. DO seat the witness so that the light, if any, falls on him is possible.
7. DO show courtesy and politeness toward the ordinary witness.
8. DO create a motive for the witness to provide you with information.
9. DO assure the witness of protection of unnecessary disclosure.
10. DO distinguish between a witness and a bias witness.
11. DO seek to identify the witness's interest with yours, in the mind of the witness.
12. DO seek to win the confidence of the witness.
13. DO obtain basic personal details from the witness.
14. DO make an investigation of the witness before interviewing, if possible.
15. DO find out where the witness may be reached, before he leaves.
16. DO impress the witness with the importance of what he has to tell you.
17. DO ascertain the sources of the witness's testimony.
18. DO attempt to determine the truthfulness of the witness's testimony.
19. DO let the witness tell his story in his own words.
20. DO make an estimate of the consistency of the witness's story.
21. DO get the witness's story before he can consult others.
22. DO attempt to ascertain the basis of the witness's recollection of important details.
23. DO question continuously--most people talk.
24. DO interview witnesses when they are "hot."
25. DO observe the behavior of the witness, his reaction to questions, his hesitancy and other qualities which characterize his responses.
26. DO note all contradictions.
27. DO obtain documentary evidence; when possible, the originals.

28. DO change interviewers, if you find that you are "stymied" with a particular witness.
29. DO remember that there are no hard and fast rules.
30. DO keep all promises made to a witness.
31. DO look the witness straight in the eye.

VI. Interviewing Don'ts

1. DON'T be rude, officious or impolite. There is <u>matter</u> in manner.
2. DON'T antagonize the witness.
3. DON'T deny or dismiss reasonable requests of the witness once he has indicated that he is cooperating.
4. DON'T interview more than one witness at a time.
5. DON'T lose control over the conduct of the interview.
6. DON'T "wisecrack" during an interview.
7. DON'T cross-examine or "grill" the witness.
8. DON'T let the witness know the purpose of the interview.
9. DON'T let suspicion fall on a witness whom you think is suspect, during an interview.
10. DON'T allow the interview to be interrupted, if you can possibly avoid it.
11. DON'T use only the question and answer type of interview.
12. DON'T lose track of, or dismiss, the witness until you have obtained from him all the information that he has.
13. DON'T ask more than one question at a time.
14. DON'T persist in following an unsuccessful approach.
15. DON'T place much credence in hearsay.
16. DON'T tell the witness what the "story" is; let <u>him</u> do the talking.
17. DON'T necessarily disbelieve an entire statement just because part of it is untrue or inaccurate.
18. DON'T ignore valid documentary evidence in favor of oral testimony.
19. DON'T assume that the witness is familiar with maps or military terminology.
20. DON'T fail to evaluate information accurately.
21. DON'T fail to obtain corroboration of testimony, if possible.
22. DON'T let the witness know how much you know.
23. DON'T lose your temper.
24. DON'T use profane language.
25. DON'T ignore your senses or common sense.
26. DON'T overlook any leads given by the witness.
27. DON'T overlook any slips made by the witness.
28. DON'T argue with the witness.
29. DON'T indulge in personalities.
30. DON'T allow the information that you get to go stale.
31. DON'T allow your prejudices against the witness, or otherwise influence your evaluation of the witness's testimony.

32. DON'T forget to note the witness's behavior and movements, i.e. any hesitation in answering questions; uneasiness; inability to maintain eye contact.
33. DON'T forget that there are no hard and fast rules to interviewing.
34. DON'T lie to the witness or make threats.
35. DON'T forget to indicate the witness's ability in your opinion to recount the incident if necessary in front of a judge and jury.

VII. Getting Started

1. Call the interviewee and introduce yourself, and explain the purpose for your call.

2. Be prepared to fully identify yourself and have a business card available.

3. Dress appropriately.

4. Make certain your batteries are charged and keep spares handy.

5. The first thing to do upon meeting the interviewee is to put him or her at ease. Don't make a big thing of your recording equipment; treat it as a natural part of the procedure. Answer any questions asked but don't volunteer unnecessary detail about what will or might be done with the recording. If pressed, you can truthfully minimize the likelihood of its use in court but make no guarantees.

6. Explain what you are going to do is to ask a few questions beforehand and then you will turn the machine on and go over the same facts.

7. Pre-interview the witness. Ask the questions you intend to ask for the record. This tends to relax the witness and also prepares you for areas of the story that you may want to go into more deeply. Before recording the statement ask the interviewee to have a pencil handy. Invite him/her to make a diagram of the accident as a guide of his/her description. This will help prevent the interviewee from contradiction.

8. It will be a good idea to tell the interviewee that some repetition will be necessary for purpose of identification and clarification.

9. Place the recording device close to the interviewee. He/she most likely will be the soft spoken one. You can always purposely speak louder.

10. If it becomes necessary to use more than one tape, make a statement to the effect at the end of each tape, identifying the tape just completed and the tape record by the number or letter at the beginning of the tape. Also make an abbreviated statement of identification.

Example: "This is (investigator's name) continuing the interview of (name). This is record #2 of the interview (date). It is (time)."

Say: "Is it correct that there was no conversation concerning this accident during the changing of the records, Mr. (Name)?"

11. Should an interruption occur by the other party or yourself, you should keep the recorder playing and comment to explain the interruption and that the recording will be continued in a few minutes.

12. If the recorder is turned off, you must ask your subject if he/she would like to discuss anything that was mentioned while the recorder was off. A few reasons for turning the machine off would be for the interviewee to answer the phone, door, clear up a complicated matter.

13. Keep each interview separate. Each interview should be a separate WAV. File.

WHILE RECORDING

1. Begin the recording by following the opening statement in the statement guide. Be sure to include the question -- "Do I have your permission to record this interview?" You must also establish that the witness understands the conversation is being recorded and that you have his permission to do so.

2. At the beginning of the statement, you should identify people, places, time and what is being done.

3. You should also establish the fact that they are giving you the statement voluntarily, without the promise of any reward and under no circumstances which would constitute a threat or duress of any kind. You need to establish the subject's educational level and their ability to read, write and understand the English language. You also need to understand and establish your subject's control of their facilities by asking if they are under the influence of any drug, alcohol or medication of any kind at the time of the taping. If they are under a doctor's care and taking some type of drug, you may want to establish what that drug is and at what time it was last taken by your subject. If, at any point and time during this statement, while your subject is providing you with specific information about circumstances which are important to your case, and you have any suspicion that the subject is taking some sort of medication, uses drugs or is a drinker, you might want to again ask him or her if at the time they observed, heard or were involved in these circumstances were they under the influence of any drugs, alcohol or medication.

4. If you are taking statements from more than one person at the same location, separate them. Do not allow one to hear the other person's statement.

5. Use good statement taking techniques during the body of the recording. Control the conversation with the aid of your statement outline. Keep the information factual and use open-end questions beginning with who, what, when, where, how, etc.

6. It is also important that you takes notes during this recorded statement. You should have also already taken notes during any statement made prior to the actual recorded statement. Both sets of notes should be available to you in order to formulate questions which will allow you to bring certain points out during the subject's statement.

1. End the recording, as suggested in the statement guide, by asking if there is anything you haven't covered, any pertinent facts, which are felt to be important. If so, let them come out freely. Then ask if he has understood all your questions and if his answers are true and correct to the best of his knowledge. Make sure the interviewee repeats his approval of having his statement recorded. A final "thank you" ends the recording.

AFTER RECORDING

1. After the recording and before you leave, run a spot-check on the record to make sure the machine was working.

2. As soon as possible, while the interview is still fresh, summarize the important facts and your impression of the witness. Indicate how the information developed in the statement may affect the client's decision to "contest" or "settle" the claim and the reasons for your conclusions. This information should be reported on in your report and comprise a vital part of the report conclusion.

3. In most cases your report will substitute for transcriptions of the recording so don't be afraid to elaborate in detail. Keep in mind that only at the request of the client will the record be transcribed.

4. Your report and the digital recording then become a "material" part of the file. The file should be saved onto to CD's one for the evidence room and the other marked and included with your report as an enclosure. Make certain the envelope is correctly labeled and sealed.

5. Remember you are not a licensed adjustor and should not be attempting to negotiate the settlement of a claim during your statement.

Please keep in mind that none of the following statement outlines in this chapter are considered to be complete and comprehensive. Each case will warrant unique questions that apply to that case alone. They are merely outlines to reference and stimulate your own question-making process.

VIII. Taking a Statement Over The Phone

It is always advised to take a statement in person so you can see the subject, study their body language and generally be more effective. However there will be cases where a statement may have to be taken over the phone. There are countless devices for taking statements over the phone from a landline. Most of these devices plug into the hand receiver and then have a separate mini jack that plugs into the recorder. When it comes to taking statement on your mobile phone, you will require an APP that allows you to download a program that will record both sides of the conversation. But some phones may not be compatible with such voice recording applications. In these cases, you will again need to rely on some hardware. Sony makes a microphone that plugs into your digital recorder on one end and an ear piece on the other. The ear piece's primary purpose is to capture the phone conversation you hear as you place your cellular phone over the ear with the microphone ear piece. The device was release in 2012 and is called the **Sony ECM-TL3 Earphone-Style Mini Electret Condenser Microphone.** I purchase my microphone ear piece on line through the Sony store for $19.99.

Of course, in Florida you still need to notify the participants before recording any phone conversations.

Even if the interview is not a formal statement, you can still tell the other party that the call is being recorded eliminating the challenges of having to write down all the information. It also prevents you from forgetting relevant data that you have to take note of when important information is being presented.

Digital Recorder

When choosing a digital recorder, I prefer those with a built in USB that allows me to just plug it into my computer and transfer and save the file. Many recorders come with a separate USB wire that just adds to the amount of stuff you need to carry or misplaced. These recorders can be found at large discount stores like WALMART or KMART from around $25.00 -$35.00. I am not a big believer in buying expensive equipment when there are so, many devices that are reasonably priced and dependable. For many years now I have used the RCA VR5220-A Digital Recorder which takes two AAA batteries and has never let me down.

Statement Report Outlines

I have enclosed just a few different sample outlines to use as a GUIDE when taking a statement. These guides DO NOT EXCEMPT you from using common sense or asking follow-up questions. Before you gout on any type of investigation, interview or statement, query your colleges, the internet or your client if they mention it for an outline. Many companies perform when you take a statement that you follow their specific outline of questions. You will eventually collect numerous statement outlines as you further your career.

   I.   Workers Compensation
   II.   Automobile
   III. Slip and Fall
   IV.   Property Theft
   V.   Auto Theft

WORKERS' COMPENSATION STATEMENT OUTLINE

In preparation of recorded statement:

Before turning on recorder socialize briefly with the subject. Advise subject that they will need their driver's license number, previous addresses, names and addresses of hospitals, doctors and therapists. Also, subject should be prepared to identify prescription drugs and frequency of use, prior employers' names and addresses and information related to any previous insurance claims. Request that the subject gather the information before you turn on the recorder. Give the subject a general overview of what to expect during the interview.

Before turning on the recorder determine if the subject is on any medication. Make sure that this medication will not effect the subject's ability to give an accurate statement.

Introduction to Statement: **Turn on Recorder**

Today's date is _____. My name is (your name) and I am employed with Claims Resource Incorporated and represent (name of insurance company). I am at (the location where you are taking the statement from). I am interviewing (name of subject) who was involved in a workers' compensation accident. (Name of claimant), are you aware that I am recording this conversation: (Response). Do I have your permission to do so? (Response).

1. Personal History

   a. What is your full name and please spell your last name?
      1. Do you have any alias or nicknames?
      2. What is your maiden name?
      3. Have you ever had your name changed?

    b. What is your current address and how long have you been living at this location?
    c. Do you own or rent? Who is responsible for the care and upkeep of your home/lawn?
    d. What is your home phone number and an emergency phone number where you can be reached?
    e. What is your previous address? Did you rent or own?
    f. What is your date and place of birth?
    g. What is your social security number and driver's license number?
    h. Do you wear glasses/contacts?
    i. Do you smoke?
    j. What is the last grade you completed (high school, technical, trade school, or college?)
    k. Are you married? If so, what is your spouse's name?
    l. Do you have any dependents? (If yes name(s) and age(s). (Do they live at home?)
    m. What is the name and address of your closest living relative?
    n. Have you ever been convicted of a crime? (If yes, date(s), location,, charges, involved in a work release program).

2. Physical Description
    a. Provide me with a physical description of yourself: Race/color, sex, age, height, weight, hair length and color, facial hair, eye color, and any other identifying characteristics.

3. Current Employment/Insured

    a. What is the name and address of your current employer/insured?
    b. How long have you been employed with your current employer?
    c. What is your job title?
    d. What are your daily duties and responsibilities? (important)
    e. Are you a direct employee or independent contractor?
    f. Was an employment application required at time of hire?
    g. What is the name of your immediate supervisor?
    h. Wages
        1. What is your rate of pay?
        2. How many hours per week do you work?
        3. How many days per week to you work?
        4. Is overtime, room, board, meals, medical insurance or other benefits provided?

4. Other Sources of Income

    a. Were you employed at a second job while working for the insured? If so are you still employed at that job? (If yes, provide details, refer to section 3h-Wages).

b. Is your spouse employed? (if yes, employer, wages and length of employment).
c. Are you receiving social security benefits, unemployment, welfare, child support, insurance benefits or any other benefits? (If yes, determine value of benefits and how long they have been receiving).
d. Do you have any other sources of income? (rental property, stocks, bonds, etc.)

5. Employment History

   a. Who have you worked for during the past five years?
      1. Location of employer
      2. Title and job duties
      3. Length of time at each job
   b. Did you serve time in the military?
      1. Military branch
      2. Date of discharge
      3. Any specialized training?
      4. Any injuries while in the military (If yes, where are the medical records kept?)

6. Off Hour Activities (Pre-Accident)

   a. Do you have any hobbies or are you involved in any sports or other recreational activities?
   b. How do you spend your free time? Organizations?
   c. What off hour activities were you involved in the two days leading up to the date of the accident? (Determine if this person could have injured himself any other way).

7. ACCIDENT (See supplement for other types of questions)

   a. What is the date, time and place of the accident? (Be specific on the location).
   b. What time did you start work on the day of the accident?
   c. What activities were you involved in at work from the time you arrived until the time of the accident?
   d. Were you performing your usual job duties at the time of the accident?
   e. In your own words tell me exactly what happened.
      (Let the subject speak freely and do not interrupt).
      Take notes and ask follow-up questions later. Make sure you understand exactly how the accident occurred before proceeding. Most important part of the statement).
   f. Exactly what were you doing when the symptoms first appeared?
   g. Did you have anything in your hands at the time of the onset of the pain?
   h. What caused the accident to occur? (Slip, fall, lifting object or blow. If slip or fall, describe exactly how you landed and on what body part).

g. Describe the pain you felt.
   1. When did you first feel the pain?
   2. What kind of pain did you feel? (Burning, dull, sharp, severe, radiating)
   3. Describe exact location of pain.
   4. Did you feel a snap, click or tearing of any part of the body? Where exactly?
   5. Was there arm or leg pain? Immediate or delayed?
   6. Did you feel a tingling present?
   7. If back injury, was there an inability to straighten up?
   8. Have you ever had similar pain or feeling? If so, when? How did it start, describe the pain or feeling and was there an medical treatment? By whom? Had it completely subsided? What caused it to reoccur? When was the last episode? Have you had continuous symptoms since then? How do they compare with the present symptoms?
   9. Had you taken any alcohol or chemical substance, prescription or otherwise into your body within 24 hours of the accident?
   10. Other than those injuries described are there any others?

8. Safety Equipment

   a. Were you using any safety devices? If yes, explain.
      1. Is the use of safety devices mandatory?
      2. Is the use of this equipment enforced?
      3. If not using, why not?

9. Witnesses

   a. Who did you first report the accident to:
      1. Name and title
      2. Date and time

   b. Was anyone working with you at the time of the accident? If yes, their title.
      1. If so, what were they doing?
      2. Were they involved in the accident or contribute to the accident in any way?

   c. Were there any other witnesses to the accident?
      1. List the names of any witnesses along with any other information that would assist us in locating these people.
      2. What was the witness doing at the time of the accident?
      3. What was the witness' reason for being in the area?

   d. Did any witness or anyone else contribute to the cause of the accident?

10. Injuries

    a. What did you do following the accident? Continue to work? Hospital?
    b. When did you first receive medical treatment? (If lapse in treatment, determine why).
    c. Who authorized medical treatment?
        1. Was a specific doctor and/or hospital recommended?
        2. What was said?
        3. Was the doctor/hospital a company approved facility?
    d. What are the name(s) of the <u>initial</u> examining and/or treating physicians?
        1. What type of treatment did you receive and what was the doctor's diagnosis?
        (Determine if x-rays were taken or any lab tests; when, where and outcome)
        2. Did you receive any medication or were you given a prescription for medication?
    e. What other doctor(s)/therapist(s) have you treated with since the time of the accident and their address.
        1. When and what treatment have you received?
        2. What was the diagnosis?
        3. Has the doctor given you any restrictions?
        4. What is your treatment program from this point forward?
        5. When is your next scheduled appointment?

11. Medication (current)

    a. Are you currently on any medication?
    b. What are you taking?
    c. What is it for? Is it working?
    d. How often do you take the medication?

12. Post Accident Activities

    a. What have your activities been since the day of the accident?
    b. What have you not been able to do since the time of the accident?
    c. When do you expect to return to work?
    d. If you are able to work in the same position, is there some other job you are capable of working?
    e. If you cannot return to this employer is there any other work you can or would like to do? Do you know where you can get that type of employment?

13. Third Party/Subrogation

    a. Was anyone else responsible for your injury? If so, why?
    b. Was accident caused by equipment failure? If yes, continue.
        1. Type of equipment, name of manufacturer, age of equipment.

  2. Any prior problems with equipment? Describe. If so, why did you continue to use it?
  3. Who is responsible for maintaining equipment?
  4. Was the equipment properly maintained?
  5. Is the maintenance service schedule available for review?
  6. Was operator (claimant or other) properly trained in the use of equipment?
  7. Were instructions being followed?
 c. If accident was caused by a third party (auto, contractor, etc.) explain.
  1. What is the name of the person or company and type of vehicle, if relevant, involved in the accident?
  2. Why were they in the area?
  3. How were they involved?
  4. Do you know the name of their insurance company. Are you contemplating a lawsuit against them?

14. Past Medical History

 a. Were you given a pre-employment physical?
 b. Do you have any pre-existing disabilities, diseases or impairments? If yes, was your employer aware of them?
  1. Who did you tell?
  2. When did you notify this person and under what circumstances?
  3. Did you list this disability/disease/ impairment on your employment application?
 c. What is the name and address of your current family physician?
 d. Have you ever had a prior injury to this body part(s) or any other body part?
 e. Have you had any prior injuries to any body part(s) that may have contributed to this accident?
 f. Have you ever had any prior injuries, diseases or surgeries? If yes, explain.
  1. Date
  2. Describe injury in detail and how it occurred.
  3. What treatment did you receive and by whom (Addresses)

15. Prior Insurance Claims

 a. Have you ever had a workers' compensation claim before? If so, provide details.
 b. Have you ever had any other type of claim(s) against an insurance company? Such as auto, slip and fall, etc. (If already covered no need to go into detail)

16. Disability

 a. What date did your current disability start and end?

b. Were you paid wages for the day of injury or any other part of your disability?

Statement Closing

Do you understand that if you work or receive income from any other source while receiving workers' compensation benefits you must immediately report the fact of the employment or monies received to the carrier or insurance company. (Response)

ASK: Is there anything else you would like to add or clarify in this statement before I conclude the recording? (If the response is no, proceed with the closing. If the response is yes, let the subject explain and ask follow-up questions if necessary. Once you are through, repeat this statement again before proceeding).

(Subject's Name), was everything you told me true and correct to the best of your knowledge and belief? (Subject's Name), were you aware that I was recording our conversation? Did I have your permission to do so? Would you please state your name for the final time? My name is (your name). Thank you for voluntarily giving this statement.

Upon request of client obtain appropriate releases

Always take a picture of the subject at the end to be inserted in the report.

AUTOMOBILE

In preparation of recorded statement:

Before turning on recorder socialize briefly with the subject. Advise subject that they will need their driver's license number, previous addresses, names and addresses of hospitals, doctors and therapists. Also, subject should be prepared to identify prescription drugs and frequency of use, prior employers' names and addresses and information related to any previous insurance claims. Request that the subject gather the information before you turn on the recorder. Give the subject a general overview of what to expect during the interview.

Before turning on the recorder determine if the subject is on any medication. Make sure that this medication will not effect the subject's ability to give an accurate statement.

Introduction to Statement: **Turn on Recorder**

Today's date is _____. My name is (your name) and I am employed with Claims Resource Incorporated and represent (name of insurance company). I am at (the location where you are taking the statement from). I am interviewing (name of subject) who was involved in an automobile accident. (Name of claimant), are you aware that I am recording this conversation: (Response). Do I have your permission to do so? (Response).

1. Personal History

    a. What is your full name and please spell your last name?
        1. Do you have any alias or nicknames?
        2. What is your maiden name?
        3. Have you ever had your name changed?
    b. What is your current address and how long have you been living at this location?
    c. Do you own or rent? Who is responsible for the care and upkeep of your home/lawn?
    d. What is your home phone number and an emergency phone number where you can be reached?
    e. What is your previous address? Did you rent or own?
    f. What is your date and place of birth?
    g. What is your social security number and driver's license number?
    h. Do you wear glasses/contacts?
    i. Do you smoke?
    j. What is the last grade you completed (high school, technical, trade school, or college?)
    k. Are you married? If so, what is your spouse's name?
    l. Do you have any dependents? (If yes name(s) and age(s). (Do they live at home?)

      m.   What is the name and address of your closest living relative?
      n.   Have you ever been convicted of a crime? (If yes, date(s), location,, charges, involved in a work release program).

2. Vehicle ID
    a. What is the year and make of the vehicle you were driving?
    b. Color?
    c. License number?
    d. Legal and registered? (also mat of other party)
    e. Was there any previous damage to your vehicle (especially if older vehicles)?

3. Scene
    a. Direction?
    b. Speed?
    c. Lane of travel?
    d. Distance when you first saw the other vehicle?
    e. The estimated speed?
    f. Direction lane?
    g. Color signal?
    h. Any skid marks left by either vehicle?
    i. Length of skids?
    j. Point of impact on the street and to the cars?
    k. Evasive action?
    l. Sudden stop - why?
    m. Were the police called?
    n. Who called them?
    o. Were there any witnesses, names, addresses, phone, statements?
    p. Were any citations issued?
    q. Arrests?
    r. Drug or alcohol involvement?
    s. Were there any visual obstructions?
    t. Any conversation after the accident with other driver?
    u. Exchange of names and addresses?
    v. Did anyone admit fault?
    w. Any corrective action taken by other vehicle?
    x. Who do you feel is at fault? Any why?

5. Passengers
    a. Number of occupants in your vehicle?
    b. Position in vehicle?
    c. Names, age address, phone.
    d. Describe them.

6. Injuries
    a. Was anyone injured?
    b. Describe injuries.

    c. Describe how injuries occurred.
    d. Did you see the accident coming?
    e. Did you brace for impact? How?
    f. Position of body and head at impact.
    g. Movement of body and head at impact.
    h. Did any body part strike interior of vehicle? Get specifics.
    i. Describe the headrests in the vehicle.
    j. Did any flying object in vehicle strike body?
    k. Did you sustain any lacerations?
    l. Bruises?
    m. Were you bleeding?
    n. Did you lose consciousness after impact? Why? How long?
    o. Were any passengers injured? (if so, ask same series of injury questions).

7. Impact
    a. Did your head hit the headrest?
    b. What was the position of your head when it hit the headrest?
    c. How far (forward, backward) did your head move at impact?
    d. Speed of vehicle at impact?
    e. Does vehicle have seat belts? Shoulder harness? Were they in use? Did the seat belt lock? Did it fail?
    f. Did seat move forward at impact?
    g. What was vehicle movement subsequent to impact? Distance traveled after impact.
    h. Does vehicle have air bag? Did it deploy?
    i. Does vehicle have impact bumper shocks?
    j. On a scale of 1 to 10, how would you rank this impact if 1 is equivalent to one car rolling into another and 10 is a head-on crash on the freeway?
    k. Did this impact resemble an experience you have had driving or otherwise? (For example, bumping into a parking curb, bumping into someone in a crowd, amusement park ride)

8. Priors
    a. Any prior injuries from accident of any type? What? When?
    b. Any prior chiro/acupuncture/PT treatment for maintenance?
    c. Over what period of time? Frequency? Diagnosis?

9. Pain at Scene
    a. When was onset of pain? Where was pain? Give comprehensive description.
    b. Ambulance requested at scene? If no, why not?
    c. Any seat belt bruises? Describe.
    d. Did you drive vehicle from scene?
    e. Did you continue to same destination?

10. Treatment

      a. Who are you seeing for this injury?
      b. Type of doctor? Type of treatment? Describe both in detail.
      c. When were you first seen?
      d. Who referred you and when? Have you ever seen this doctor before for any reason?
      e. Who administers the treatment and how long does it last?
      f. Do you use a sign-in sheet?
      g. Who is paying for TX? Do you know how much the bill is?
      h. Who is your regular family doctor? (GYN, Pediatrician)
      i. Are you work disabled? Period of time? Describe restrictions.
      j. Is therapy helping you to return to pre-accident status?
      k. Any permanency expected?
      l. If late treatment, explain why.
      m. Have injuries changed lifestyle? Sports, aerobics, church, amusement, shopping?
      n. Is there anything you can't do today that you were able to do before this accident?

11. Claim Information
      a. Have you reported this to your insurance company? (rule out duplicate property damage claims). If so, what carrier and policy number?

12. Closing

Do you understand that if you work or receive income from any other source while receiving workers' compensation benefits you must immediately report the fact of the employment or monies received to the carrier or insurance company. (Response)

ASK: Is there anything else you would like to add or clarify in this statement before I conclude the recording? (If the response is no, proceed with the closing. If the response is yes, let the subject explain and ask follow-up questions if necessary. Once you are through, repeat this statement again before proceeding).

(Subject's Name), was everything you told me true and correct to the best of your knowledge and belief? (Subject's Name), were you aware that I was recording our conversation? Did I have your permission to do so? Would you please state your name for the final time? My name is (your name). Thank you for voluntarily giving this statement.

Upon request of client obtain appropriate releases

Obtain a photograph of subject to be inserted in the report

SLIP/FALL STATEMENT
(Fall Down Cases)

1. Today's date is Month/Day/Year. My name is (your name) and I am employed with Claims Resource Incorporated and represent (name of insurance company). I am at (the location where you are taking the statement from). I am interviewing (name of subject) who was involved in an accident. (Name of claimant), are you aware that I am recording this conversation: (Response). Do I have your permission to do so? (Response).

2. Identify claimant:

    a. Name, age, address, marital status, phone, etc.
    b. Occupation and address, phone, salary, etc.
    c. Other insurance benefits -- names of companies and benefits. (Exclude from s/s).

3. Why claimant at scene:

    a. Guest? Details of visit.
    b. Licensee? Details of purpose of visit.
    c. Invitee? Details of purpose of visit.
    d. Trespasser? Details of entrance upon the premises.
    e. A minor? Attractive nuisance doctrine possibilities.
    f. Landlord - Tenant relationship.
    g. Employer - Employee relationship.

4. Location of accident:

    a. Common stairway or private?
    b. Sidewalk? Public or private?
    c. Apartment building and leases, if any, involved?
    d. How often was claimant there before? Last specific date of visit?

5. Defects:

    a. Negate, if none.
    b. Did claimant see of know of defect. Describe defect and location.
    c. Was defect present last time claimant was there? Date.
    d. Did defect cause accident?
    e. Did insured know of defect? If so, when? What did he do about correcting it or protecting others from its potential danger?

6. Lighting.

a. Artificial: Adequate? Type? Number and positions in relation to point of fall down?
   b. Natural: Enough? Not enough?
   c. Did lighting show up defects?
   d. Did lack of light cause accident?

7. Other important facts:

   a. Bannister there? Was it used?
   b. Type of shoes worn? Type soles? Type heels?
   c. Claimant in a hurry? If so, why?
   d. Claimant carrying anything? What? How or in what manner?
   e. Admissions made by insured and claimant at time of accident? Describe.

8. Precise location of fall:

   a. Exact step claimant fell on?
   b. Exact spot in walk claimant fell?

9. Description of fall:

   a. Feet slip out from under?
   b. Fell forward?
   c. Twisted ankle?
   d. Other possible ways claimant fell.
   e. How did claimant land?

10. Injury sustained:

    a. Did defect cause injury? Describe claimant's symptoms and complaints in detail. Identity of claimant's doctor, hospital, type of treatment given and cost to date.

    b. Did claimant ever injure this part of body before? History of past injury, names of hospitals he was in, names and addresses of doctors who rendered any services, etc.

11. Identify all witnesses:

    a. Impartial?
    b. Bias? Accompanying claimant?
    c. After witnesses.

12. Closing:

>ASK: Is there anything else you would like to add or clarify in this statement before I conclude the recording? (If the response is no, proceed with the closing. If the response is yes, let the subject explain and ask follow-up questions if necessary. Once you are through, repeat this statement again before proceeding).
>
>(Subject's Name), was everything you told me true and correct to the best of your knowledge and belief? (Subject's Name), were you aware that I was recording our conversation? Did I have your permission to do so? Would you please state your name for the final time? My name is (your name). Thank you for voluntarily giving this statement.
>
>For written statements have interviewee "initial" each page, and include on last page acknowledgement, "I have read the above report of _____ pages and it is true and correct to the best of my knowledge and belief." Have interviewee also check to be certain that all errors have been initialed and sign last page.
>
>(BI Claimant, obtain Medical and Employment Authorizations.) After statement, it may be requested that you obtain Medical and Employee Wage Authorizations.

PROPERTY THEFT STATEMENT

1. Today's date is Month/Day/Year. My name is (your name) and I am employed with Claims Resource Incorporated and represent (name of insurance company). I am at (the location where you are taking the statement from). I am interviewing (name of subject) who reported a property theft. (Name of claimant), are you aware that I am recording this conversation: (Response). Do I have your permission to do so? (Response).

2. Personal Data on Insured:

   a. Name, address, and home phone number of insured.
   b. Type of work, where employed, and length of employment.
   c. Name of spouse.
   d. Spouse's type of work, where employed, and length of employment.

3. Description of Incident:

   Ask the insured to describe in his own words each of the following: the stolen object, the time and location of the theft, and how entry was gained (where applicable). Then ask any of the following which you need to get a full picture of the incident.

4. Circumstances Surrounding Theft:

   a. Location from which property was taken.
   b. Who left it there?
   c. When and why was it left there?
   d. When was property last seen?
   e. How was property taken?
   f. By whom and when was loss discovered?
   g. Where was insured at time of loss?
   h. Did stolen property have any business use? If so, what?
   i. Any unusual occurrences prior to loss.

5. Structure Burglarized:

   a. If house burglarized:

      1. Was dwelling the insured's home? If not, why was he there?
      2. Type of dwelling.
      3. Number of residents, their relation to insured.
      4. Were all doors and windows locked?
      5. How was entry gained?
      6. Any damage to dwelling? Are repairs needed?
      7. Who has access to building?

b. If garage or other outbuilding burglarized:

   1. Location of building.
   2. Were all doors and windows locked?
   3. How was entry gained?
   4. Are repairs needed?
   5. Who has access to building?

c. If apartment burglarized:

   1. On which floor is apartment located?
   2. Number of apartments on same floor; number in building.
   3. Number of entrances to apartment; number in building.
   4. Were doors and windows of apartment locked?
   5. How was entry gained?
   6. Any damage to apartment?
   7. Who has keys to apartment?
   8. Any security system?

6. Police Report:

   a. Which police department wrote report?
   b. Case number.
   c. Name of investigating officer.
   d. Time at which police were called.
   e. Was investigation performed at scene?
   f. Did detectives follow-up?
   g. Were evidence tests performed, e.g. fingerprints, etc.?
   h. Were neighbors interviewed?
   i. Other recent burglaries in area?
   j. Was complete inventory taken?

7. Loss Evaluation:

   a. For all items, establish: brand, serial number, cost, place and date of purchase, and estimated current value.
   b. Are receipts available?
   c. Is this inventory complete?
   d. Has a thorough search been made for all items?
   e. Have all items been reported to police?
   f. Does insured own all items?
   g. If not, who does?
   h. Any of missing items financed?
   i. If so, with whom, what account number?
   j. Any other insured on items? If so, name of carrier, policy number.

8. Insurance History:

  a. Has insured had prior theft losses?
  b. Time and circumstances of such losses.
  c. Name and carrier at that time, policy number

9. Statement Closing

ASK: Is there anything else you would like to add or clarify in this statement before I conclude the recording? (If the response is no, proceed with the closing. If the response is yes, let the subject explain and ask follow-up questions if necessary. Once you are through, repeat this statement again before proceeding).

  (Subject's Name), was everything you told me true and correct to the best of your knowledge and belief? (Subject's Name), were you aware that I was recording our conversation? Did I have your permission to do so? Would you please state your name for the final time? My name is (your name). Thank you for voluntarily giving this statement.

  For written statements have interviewee "initial" each page, and include on last page acknowledgement, "I have read the above report of _____ pages and it is true and correct to the best of my knowledge and belief." Have interviewee also check to be certain that all errors have been initialed and sign last page.

AUTO THEFT STATEMENT OUTLINE

In preparation of recorded statement:

Before turning on the recorder socialize briefly with the subject. Advise the subject that they will need their driver's license number, previous addresses, names and addresses of hospitals, doctors and therapists. Also, subject should be prepared to identify prescription drugs and frequency of use, prior employers' names and addresses and information related to any previous insurance claims. Request that the subject gather the information before you turn on the recorder. Give the subject a general overview of what to expect during the interview.

Before turning on the recorder determine if the subject is on any medication. Make sure that this medication will not affect the subject's ability to give an accurate statement.

Introduction to Statement: **Turn on Recorder**

Today's date is _____. My name is (your name) and I am employed with Claims Resource Incorporated and represent (name of insurance company). I am at (the location where you are taking the statement from). I am interviewing (name of subject) who was reported a vehicle theft. (Name of claimant), are you aware that I am recording this conversation: (Response). Do I have your permission to do so? (Response).

1. Personal History

    a. What is your full name and please spell your last name?
       1. Do you have any alias or nicknames?
       2. What is your maiden name?
       3. Have you ever had your name changed?
    b. What is your current address and how long have you been living at this location?
    c. Do you own or rent? Who is responsible for the care and upkeep of your home/lawn?
    d. What is your home phone number and an emergency phone number where you can be reached?
    e. What is your previous address? Did you rent or own?
    f. What is your date and place of birth?
    g. What is your social security number and driver's license number?
    h. Do you wear corrective lens? glasses/contacts
    i. Do you smoke?
    j. What is the last grade you completed (high school, technical, trade school, or college?)
    k. Are you married? If so, what is your spouse's name?
    l. Do you have any dependents? (If yes name(s) and age(s). (Do they live at home?)

    m. What is the name and address of your closest living relative?
    n. Have you ever been convicted of a crime? (If yes, date(s), location,, charges, involved in a work release program).

3. Current Employment

    a. What is the name and address of your current employer
    b. How long have you been employed with your current employer?
    c. What is your job title?
    d. What is your working schedule-from what time to what time? What days each week?
    e. How do you usually get to work?

4. Residential and Vehicle Information

    a. How many cars do you own at the present time?
    List all:
    make/model/color/tag numbers/INSURANCE CARRIERS
    b. Do you have anyone else living with you? If yes identify vehicles owned.
    c. Do you have any renters? If yes identify vehicles
    d. Where do you park each car? Describe parking location.

5. Stolen Vehicle/Loss

    a. Identify the vehicle stolen.
        1. year
        2. make/model/color
        3. VIN (Vehicle Identification Number?)
        4. mileage
        5. extra equipment?
            a. CB
            b. CD changer
            c. Post factory Stereo system
            d. ALARM? If so what type?
                1. Any theft warranty/guarantee?
                2. Was it on? if so how does subject explain theft?
                    a. Was there an ignition disabling feature in alarm package?
                    b. Have any other break-ins or theft occurred while this alarm was on? If so was it reported to the police? When, where and what date(s)
                3. If not on why not?
        6. Tag number and State of issue
        7. Any Stickers or Decals? Description and location.
        8. Describe dents, dings, scrapes, scratches, broken glass, missing parts or any other markings.
    b. What was this car used for? work? if so what is distance?
    c. Where is it normally parked?

- d. How many sets of keys are there to this vehicle? Any missing?
- e. Who ALL drives this or has access to it?
- f. Who used the car last, immediately prior to theft?
- g. List all other possible drivers
    - a. spouse, children, friends, co-employees, etc..
- h. Where and when was car last seen? By whom?
    - a. When was gas last put in vehicle? Any receipt?
- i. What if any personal property was inside the car - full description
    1. Brand, serial number, cost, place, date of purchase, method of payment and estimated current value.
    2. Are receipts available?
    3. Is the inventory sent to the Insurance Company complete?
    4. What inventory was identified in the police report? Is there any different between the two if so why? and have the police been re-contacted to up date police report?
    5. Has a thorough search for the items been made?
    6. Does the insured own all the items?
    7. Any of the missing items financed? If so with whom and what account numbers?
    8. Any other insurance on items? Is so, name of carrier, policy number

- j. What was in the glove box? Trunk?
- k. Was this cars registration current?
- l. Was ignition locked when car was left? Where doors locked? Windows locked?
- m. Were there any keys hidden in or outside the car?
- n. Do you have other transportation available to you?
    1. Second car?
    2. Car Pool possibility
    3. Friends, co-worker in area?
    4. Taxi, Buses?
- o. When will alternate transportation be required?
- p. What arrangements have been made?

6. Incident/Loss

    a. Where were you going at the time you discovered the loss? Or where were you coming from?
    b. Was this a planned trip or a normal everyday event?
    c. Did you plan to leave at this time? If so what plans where made? Anything special or out of the ordinary?
        1. On vacation leaving town? Had Hotel reservations etc.?
    d. Do you have any idea who might have stolen the car?
    e. Do the police have any suspects?
    f. How was the car broken into? Any keys missing?
    g. Who first discovered the car was missing?
        1. What time was this?

2. What date?
   e. What did you do next? Call Police? Call insurance company?
   f. Was the vehicle recovered? If so who found it?
      a. how were you notified?
      b. Was there any personal property still in the vehicle?
   g. Did you speak to any neighbors?
   h. Had anyone seen or heard anything relating to the loss, i.e. neighbor heard glass break at ? time, etc?
   i. Was anyone with you or outside at the time you discovered your vehicle missing? Obtain description name and address of witnesses.
   j. What was your reaction? What did you think of at that moment?
   k. What were you doing just prior to finding the loss.

8. Police
   a. Who called the police?
   b. What time was this done?
   c. What time did the Police arrive?
   d. What Police Agency responded?
      a. Police Officers Name
      b. Badge Number?
   c. Case Number
   e. Who filled out or was interviewed by the officer for official report?
   f. Did you hand write your own statement?
   g. How much time did you take to prepare a statement to the police?
   h. Was a list of the personal items in the vehicle given at the time the police officer arrived?
   i. How much time did you have to gather these items?
   j. Did the Police perform an investigation at the scene?
   k. Did detectives follow-up?
   l. Were any evidence tests performed, i.e., finger prints, etc.?
   m. Did the police interview neighbors?
   n. Other recent Burglaries in area?
   o. Was a complete inventory taken?

12. Post Incident Activities
    a. Did you eventual leave for your original destination once the police and Insurance company were notified? Did you go to work?
    b. What transportation did you use?
    c. What time did you eventually leave?
    d. Has any of the personal property been replaced?
       1. Do you have the receipts for those items replaced by you?

13. History of Vehicle

    a. When was vehicle purchased?
    b. From Whom? Full name and address
    c. Cost?

d. Any Trade-In? Is so describe trade-in and allowance.
  e. Do you have a copy of the sales contract? Could you get a copy?
  f. Method of Payment?
     1. Down payment
     2. financed? through who? terms?
     3. Monthly payments?
     4. Are payments up to date?
     5. What is your balance
     6. Will your insurance cover your amount owed on vehicle?
     7. Is insurance included in your financing?
     8. Monthly cost of Insurance?
  g. How long have you had Insurance on your vehicle?
  h. Was there any prior insurance coverage on this vehicle with another carrier?
  i. Have any prior claims for loss associated with this car been made to another Insurance Company?
  j. Have you had any prior reported theft losses? If so what carrier and Police was this reported to?
  k. Was normal maintenance performed as suggested by Owners Manual?
  l. Who has performed maintenance on this vehicle? Name and address of Dealer, Garage and Mechanic.
  m. What was the date of the last service?
  n. What service was performed? Amount?
  o. Any more recent mechanical/cosmetic problems with vehicle?
  p. Was this car ever in an Accident? If so where were Mechanical and Body repairs made?
     1. What carrier was claim submitted to?
     2. Was a police report filed? If so where and what date?
  q. Was any new item recently purchased for the car? If so, what and where is it now? Car bra, stereo, seat covers, etc?
     1. Any receipts for items?

14. Prior Insurance Claims
   a. Have you ever had any type of theft claim before? If so, provide details.
   b. Have you ever had any other type of claim(s) against an insurance company?

Statement Closing

ASK: Is there anything else you would like to add or clarify in this statement before I conclude the recording? (If the response if no, proceed with the closing. If the response is yes, let the subject explain and ask follow-up questions if necessary. Once you are through, repeat this statement again before proceeding).

(Subject's Name), was everything you told me true and correct to the best of your knowledge and belief? (Subject's Name), were you aware that I was recording our conversation? Did I have your permission to do so? Would you please state your name for the final time? My name is (your name). Thank you for voluntarily giving this statement.

Chapter Fifteen
Preparing for A PI Position

   I. Introduction
   II. Your Resume
   III. What type of Job Am I Interviewing For

15. Introduction

Our goal is provide you with useful information that will help you in your pursuit of a career in Private investigations. And, of course interviewing for a job will be essential and many companies have assessment tests to calculate how well you know the industry.

Part of the process will be how well you can compile your thoughts and whether these thoughts are *adapted to the reader based on the facts of the case.*

One of the entry level tests is for the applicant to watch video taken by a surveillance investigator. You watch the film and then report on what you saw. Sounds simple right!

Well let's say you should at least practice this on your own and look for any mistakes or ways to make your report more concise. Maybe your choice of words can be improved so take some video then write out what you saw (based on the reason for the footage) and let someone else read what you wrote and critique your report.

So after you shoot some video, type up a brief paragraph describing your observations to see how well you can recall and describe what you saw. Don't keep going back to the video, look at it once, make notes, then, write. If you are doing an Insurance Surveillance on an injured person, your details should relate to the physical movements and noted capacity of the individual with a direct focus on their injury and how it may or may not impact the activity observed.

Along with checking your detail and writing ability, an employer they will also want to gage your knowledge of the industry through questions regarding privacy issues, the use of pretexts, different types of investigations, procedures and industry specific terminology. A classroom education can only teach you so much and there is no replacement for actual field experience. There is no doubt the more you work in the field, the better acclimated you become to the over all work of an Investigator. Surveillance, one of the largest fields in our industry is an art that you will perfect through repetition and practice. Getting use to using your camera will improve your surveillance results. The quicker you can pick-up, turn on and focus your camera will enable you to secure better quality footage. It is not uncommon to take your camera to a supermarket or busy commercial location and attempt to video the subjects going into the store and then exiting. I would suggest you spend several hours each weekend shooting video and then review the video and critique it. Look for how shaky the video may be. Do you start and stop the video? Is the video clear, is the subject in the full screen with his head at the top of the screen and his feet at the bottom, are parts of your car in the video? Did you have to move around the parking lot to get the best video possible? How did you prepare for when the subject exited the store?

The next step in your training is to then go to a neighborhood and start to follow a random person out of the neighborhood and see where they go. If they stop at a convenience store are you able to start your filming just before they exit their vehicle? If not what can you do to increase your ready speed. Getting video of a person exiting their vehicle and going into a store is a crucial piece of documentation a seasoned investigator will obtain and something a client will look for to access your talent.

An experienced manager can tell how long you have been in the field just by reviewing your video. Perhaps even worst is that when we see less than acceptable video, we think one of two things, this person is new or the worst case scenario, this person doesn't care about their work product. Therefore your final product is very important. As you start out focus on quality NOT quantity, five minutes of great video is better than 10 minutes of blurry or out of focus or shaky video.

Your Resume

Having hired hundreds of investigators, I can tell you that hiring managers usually spend about ten seconds looking at your resume. Make sure the Resume is no longer than one page. Your goal is to get an interview not tell your whole life story on paper (which won't be read and really makes you look bad). In our business simple and to the point is better. Don't send a copy of your Investigative Certificates, Diplomas, Driver's License or any other documentation unless they ask for it specifically.

Make sure the resume is typed and an original copy or printed copy. Don't send photocopies of your resume. Have your resume printed on nice neutral color paper. If you use a number make sure you answer that number not a house phone that you never answer. Same goes with the email address, check it often. Most employers will call you to discuss your resume and then decide if they want to proceed further. Again keep the conversation professional, you still need to get in front for the hiring manager. The more versatile you are the more attractive you appear to the employer. You need to realize you may be needed in another town or that a lot of driving is required. There is also probably 50 people applying for the same job you are so understand that its not what the company can do for you its what can you do for the company. You need to get use to this concept because this is a performance oriented business. High pressure, results oriented and no complaining or excuses.

Being a PI is a lot like being an entrepreneur, you need to be resourceful, independent and results oriented. Anyone that requires a lot of hand holding or doesn't understand how to get results wont last in the industry. But don't be afraid by all of this tough talk, you'll get the hang of it but you need to stay focused and work hard. You may find yourself spending more time to get something right than originally expected. There is nothing wrong with putting in extra time to learn.

Resume

Joe Davis
1915 Eastview Drive, Sun City Center, FL 33573
Telephone 706.399.9753 / Email DavisJ@email.sc.edu

Objective: Secure a position with a Private Investigative Agency or Insurance SIU department specializing in Claims Investigations and Surveillance. Utilize my passion for investigative work and desire to outperform expectations and deliver results.

Education: City College 8/2014
A.S. Private Investigations

Experience: Private Investigator's Class "CC" license 8/2012.

Courses Taken:

- Surveillance Procedures and techniques
- Locate procedures
- Statement Taking
- Taking Clear, Steady Video and Video Capture
- Report Writing and Embedding Pictures in Report
- 493 Rules, Procedures and Regulations
- Legal Issues of the Professional Investigator
- Equipment, Surveillance Camera and Covert Gear
- Being a Witness and Testifying

Ranked Top 10 Student

References: Al's American Bail Bonds, Plant City
Allen McCoy 813.546.1376

What Type of Job Am I Interviewing For?

In the prior chapters, I have talked about some of the different types of cases the professional PI conducts. Some Agencies you apply to will be general PI Agencies and cover all aspects of the business. These are usually smaller companies that rely on a broad spectrum of work options to keep their investigators busy and the cases coming in. Others will specialize in Insurance Claim Work or Criminal and Civil Defense. Go on-line and review the Agencies web-site and spend time researching the meaning of any content you read.

The more professional agencies typically look to specialize in one aspect of the industry. Specialization enables the investigator to concentrate and improve in the overall quality of the product they deliver. Improving your service is and should be an on-going priority of the professional investigator. Do you deliver a professional looking report? Do you enclose pictures in your report? Do you use an on-line system to track and deliver your product to the client? Does the client have access to your files/reports 24/7? Is your equipment up to date or is there a product that will improve the look or quality of your investigation. A good quality camera IS IMPORTANT. So is a back-up camera and a reliable covert camera. These are basic pieces of equipment that keep getting better with new technology. Something as simple as having a digital tape recorder that can deliver .wav file of your statements by email to your client or a printer that prints your logo labels on your DVDs all improve the look and quality of service you offer.

And finally, remember customer service is everything. Treat your clients like gold and deliver results. Clients are hard to come by and it costs more money to look for new clients than does to keep the ones you have satisfied.

Good luck and happy hunting!

Author

John Bilyk has been a career Private Investigator for over 30 years. Originally from Philadelphia, he graduated from West Chester University with a degree in Criminal Justice. He joined a Private Investigative Firm 1982, specializing in Insurance Claims Investigations. He has worked, directed or supervised more than 50,000 cases and is considered an Expert in Claims Investigations and Surveillance.

John Bilyk has always been a strong believer in continuing education. He attained his Certified Fraud Examiner designation, CFE status in 1995. He was licensed and practiced as a PI in 12 States throughout the U.S. and the Commonwealth of Puerto Rico. With offices throughout the country he understands the challenge of operating a multi-state operation dealing with varying states rules, regulations and compliance issues.

As a Director and Board Member, he organized the first Associates Degree program in Florida for Private Investigations through the Institute of Specialized Training and Management (ISTM).

As a lifelong Private Investigator he is devoted to the private investigations industry, teaching, writing and training. He has trained hundreds of investigators who have made Private Investigations their career.

This book was written to provide an exploratory look at the PI business based on Mr. Bilyk's personal business experience.

"The decision to become a Private Investigator was a life long dream and an overwhelmingly satisfying career. I hope you too can enjoy the same success and wish you the best in your endeavor".

John C. Bilyk Jr., CFE

www.ingramcontent.com/pod-product-compliance
Lightning Source LLC
Chambersburg PA
CBHW041122300426
44113CB00002B/30